W9-ART-526

You are Home

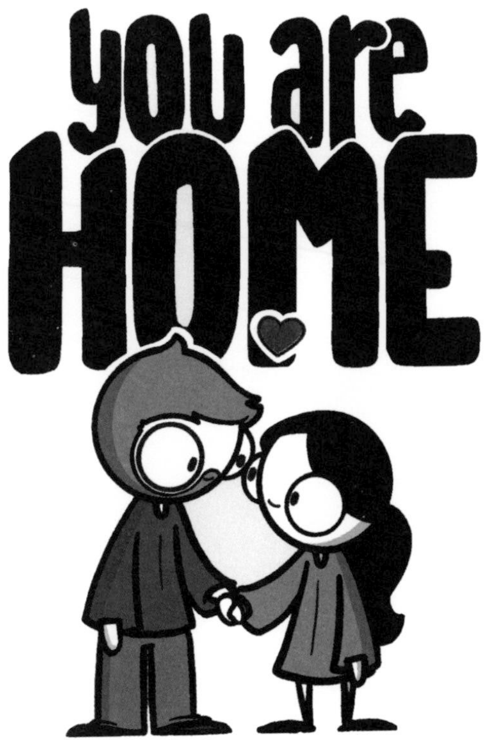

You Are Home

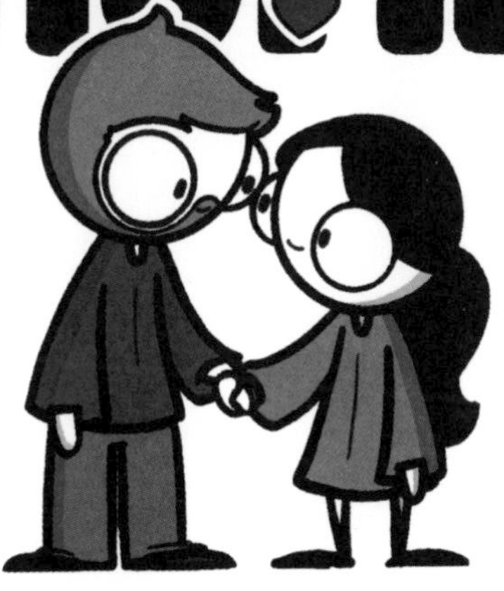

a catana comics collection

CATANA CHETWYND

Andrews McMeel
PUBLISHING®

INTRODUCTION

For a long time, I hadn't known that *home* could feel like a person. Well, more than a person, but specifically a *bond* with a person. Within our bond—our friendship, our relationship—I feel at home. No matter where we are, no matter what happens, this will always be true. It's a feeling of relief in their presence, of guard-down-ness, the feeling of being in your own space in your comfiest clothes.

This comic collection is a testament to that homey bond—both being at home together and finding home in each other. We know so many people feel this way, so it is an honor to be able to illustrate it. We hope you see yourselves in this book and can follow along with us. This book is for you and your home! We couldn't be more excited for you to read it.

Catana

our texts before living together

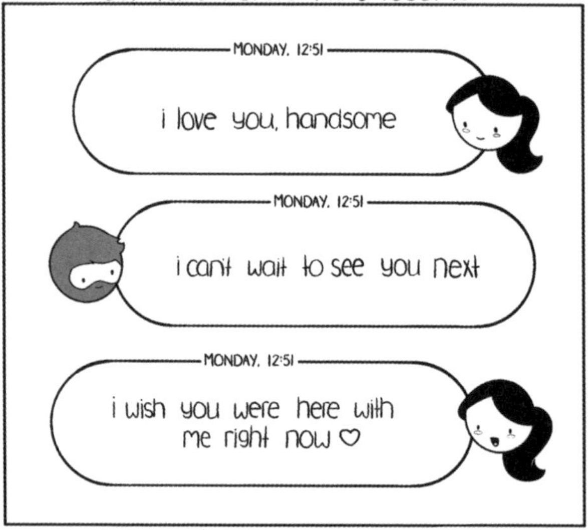
MONDAY, 12:51
i love you, handsome
MONDAY, 12:51
i can't wait to see you next
MONDAY, 12:51
i wish you were here with me right now ♡

our texts after living together

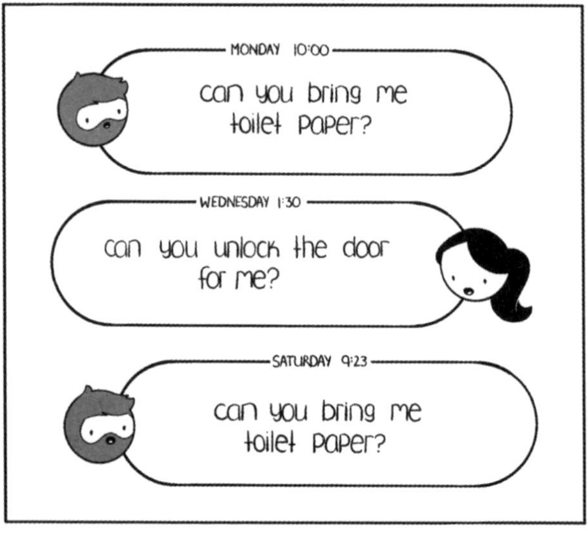
MONDAY 10:00
can you bring me toilet paper?
WEDNESDAY 1:30
can you unlock the door for me?
SATURDAY 9:23
can you bring me toilet paper?

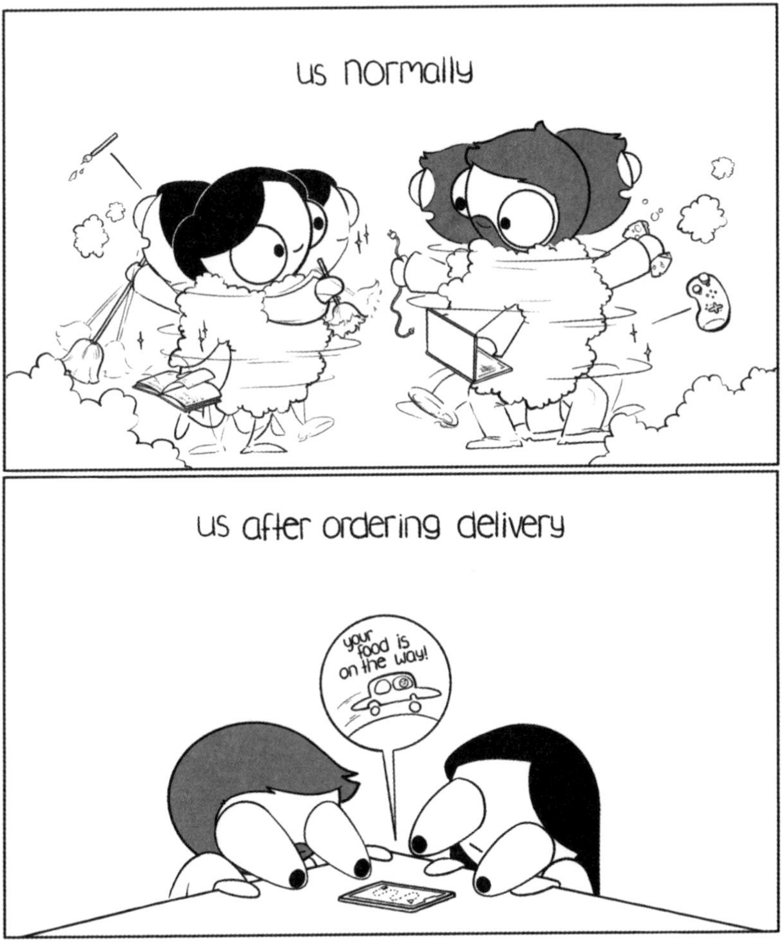
us normally
us after ordering delivery
your food is on the way!

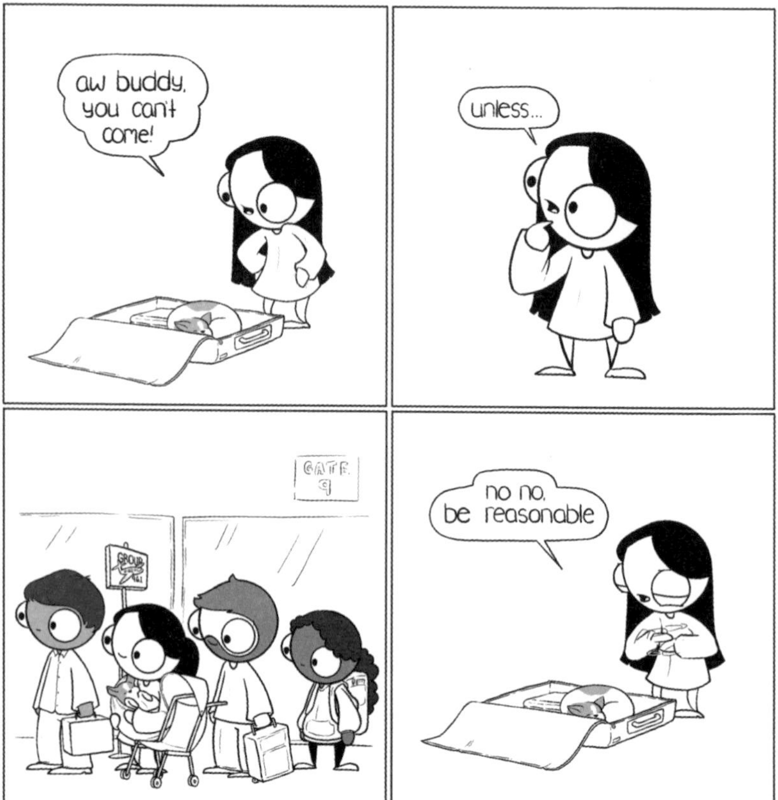
aw buddy,
you can't
come!
unless...
GATE
9
GROUP
no no,
be reasonable

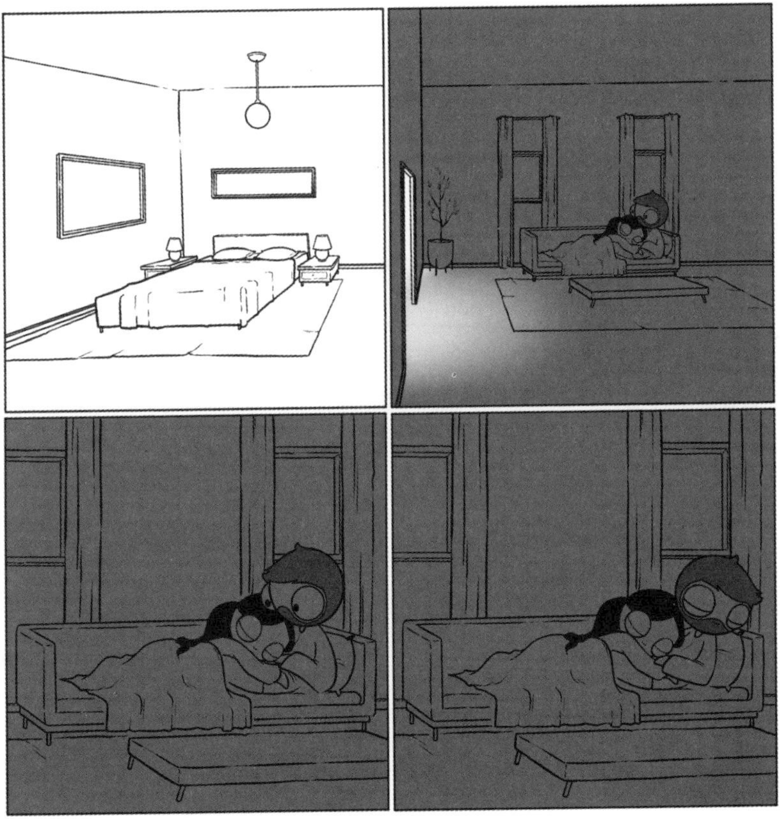

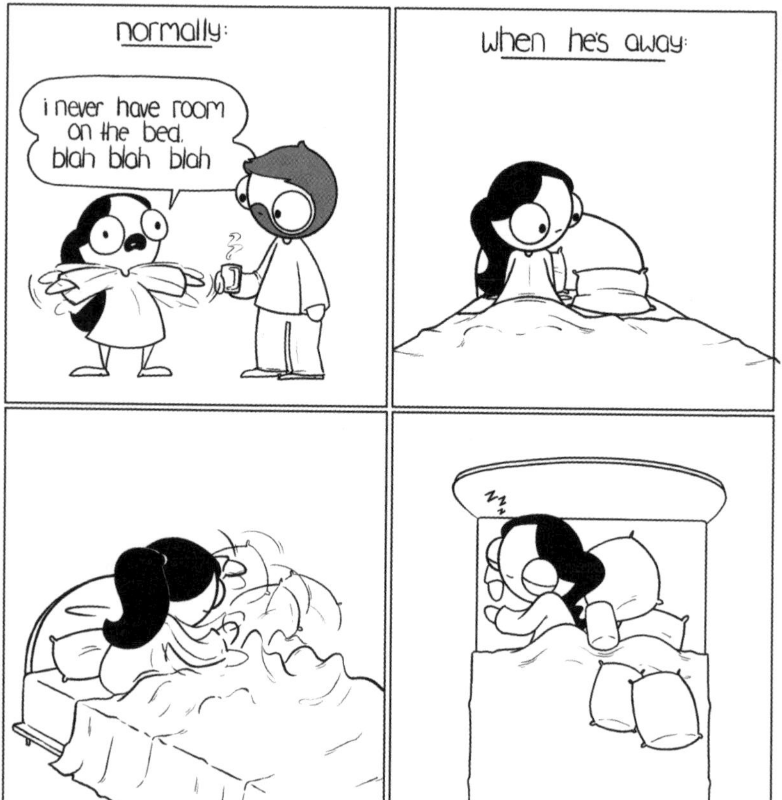
normally:
i never have room on the bed. blah blah blah
when he's away:
zzz

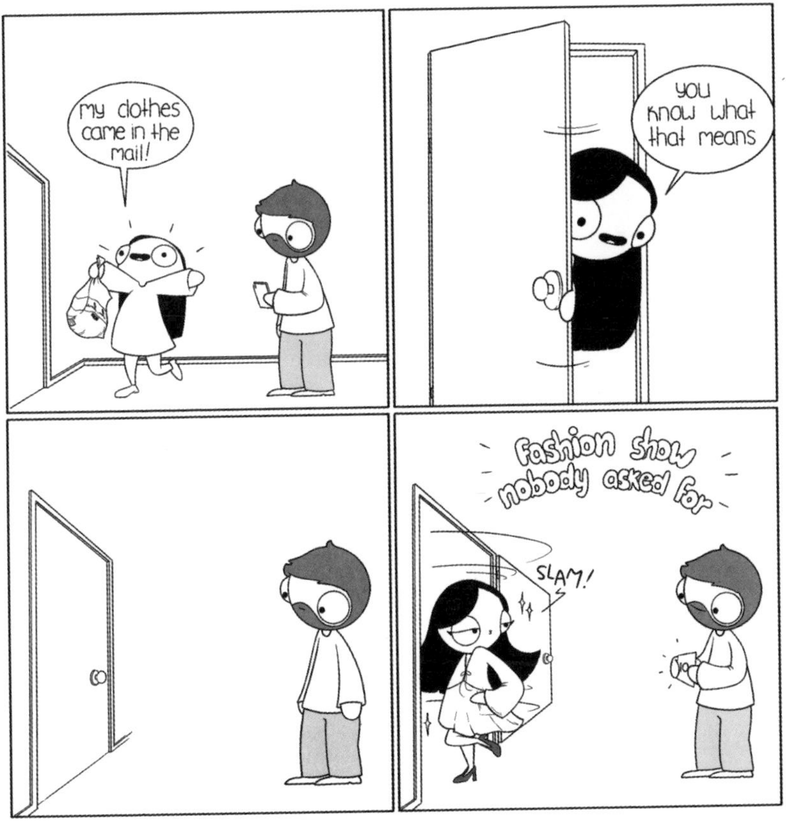
my clothes came in the mail!
you know what that means
Fashion show nobody asked for
SLAM!

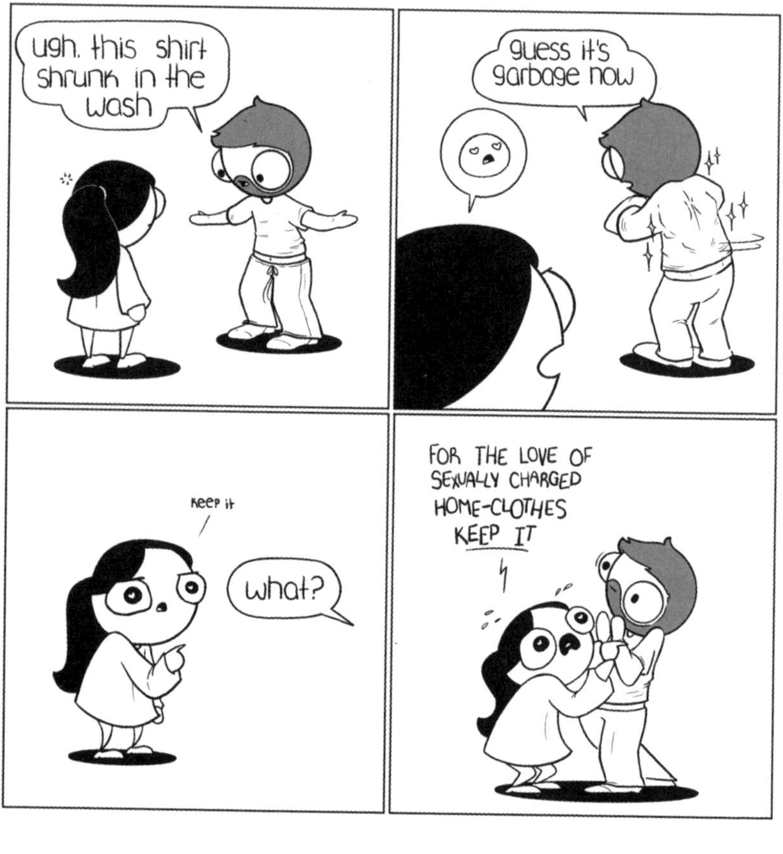
ugh. this shirt shrunk in the wash
guess it's garbage now
keep it
what?
FOR THE LOVE OF SEXUALLY CHARGED HOME-CLOTHES KEEP IT

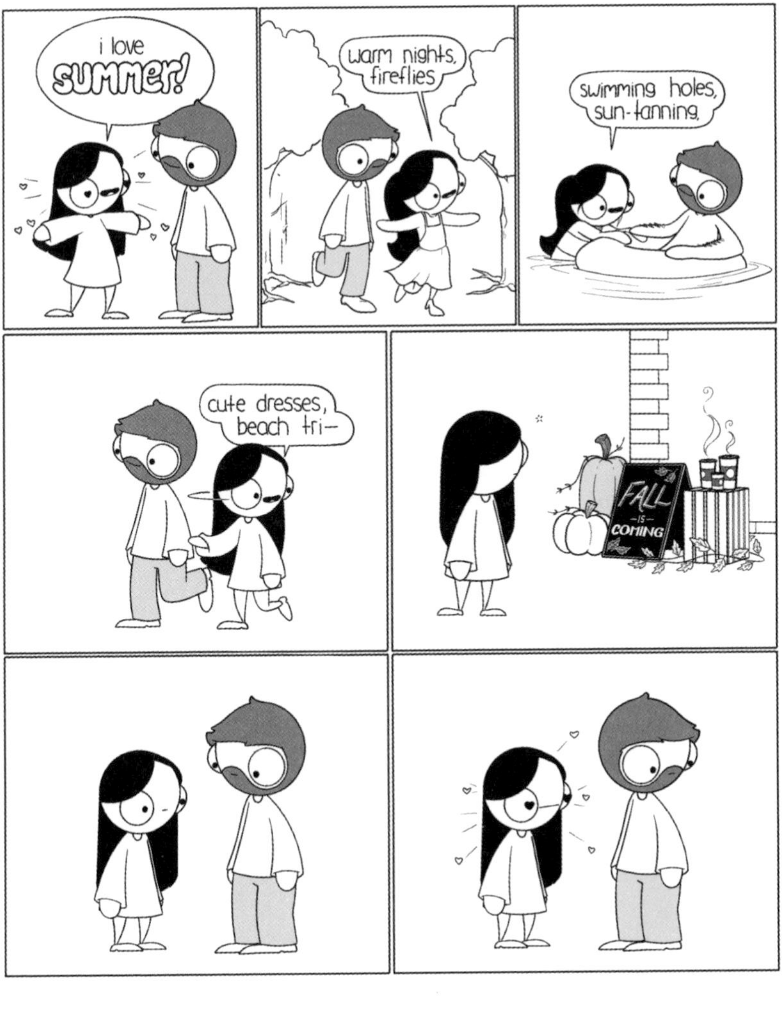
i love
SUMMER!
warm nights,
fireflies
swimming holes,
sun-tanning,
cute dresses,
beach tri—
FALL
IS
COMING

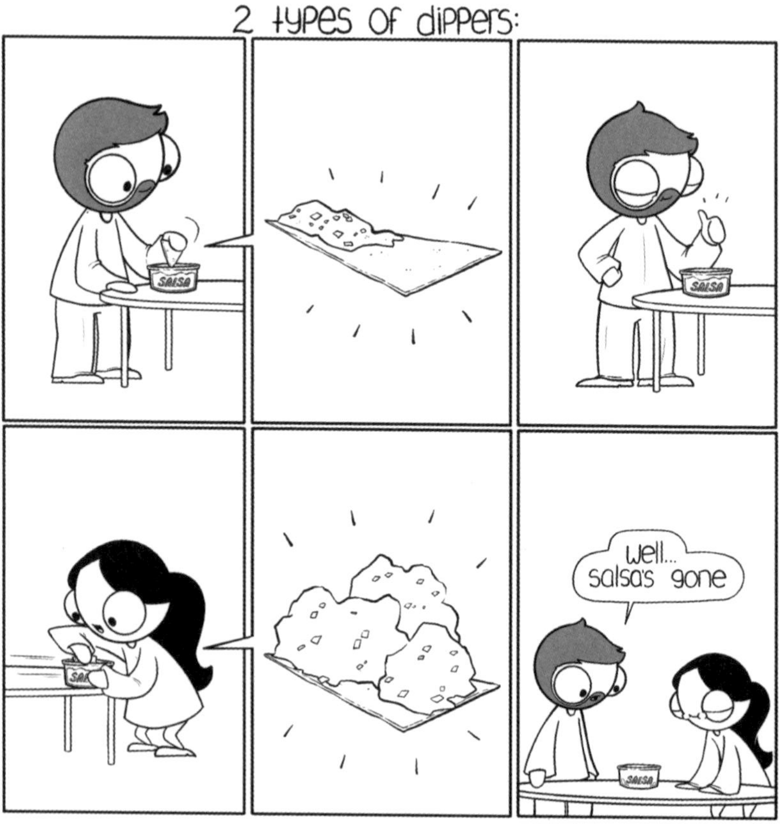
2 types of dippers:
SALSA
SALSA
well...
salsa's gone
SALSA

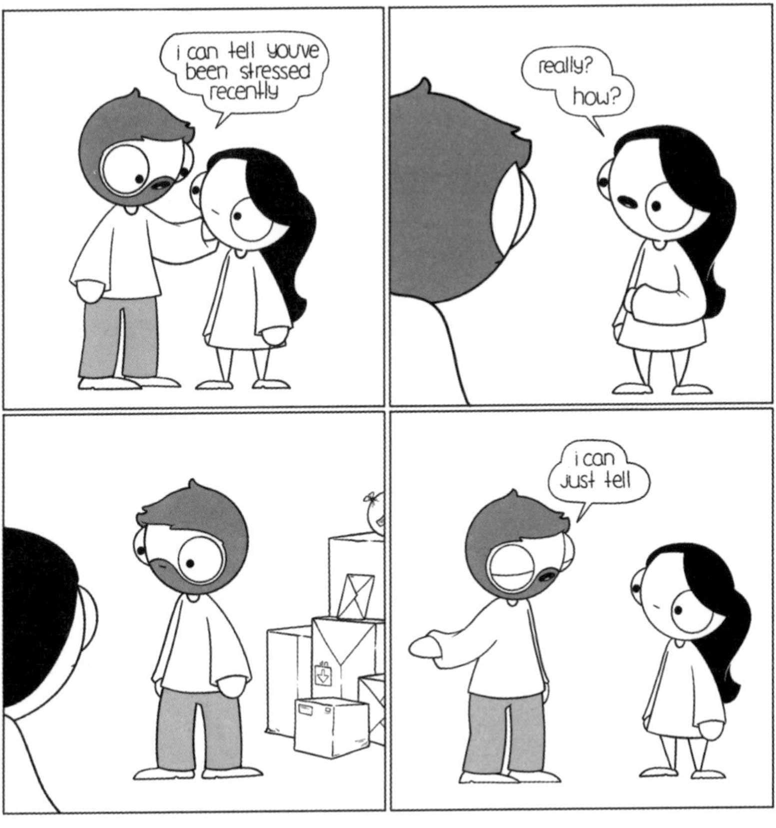
i can tell you've been stressed recently
really?
how?
i can just tell

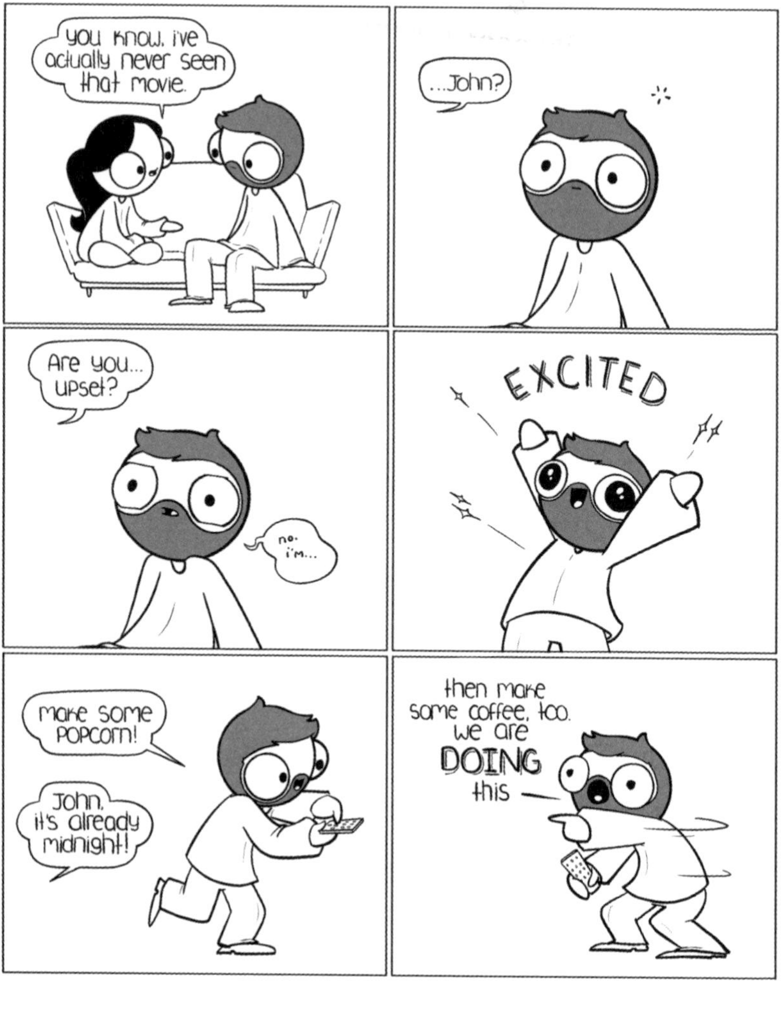
you know, i've actually never seen that movie.
...John?
Are you... upset?
no. i'm...
EXCITED
make some POPCORN!
John, it's already midnight!
then make some coffee, too. we are DOING this

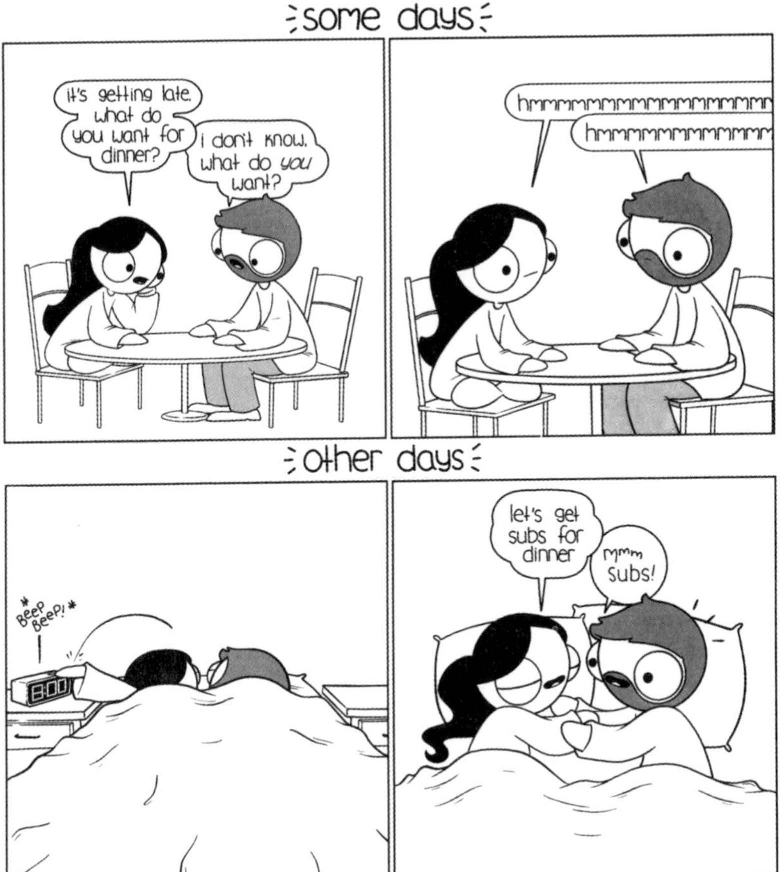
some days
it's getting late. what do you want for dinner?
i don't know. what do *you* want?
hmmmmmmmmmmmmmmmm
hmmmmmmmmmmmm
other days
BEEP BEEP!
let's get subs for dinner
mmm subs!

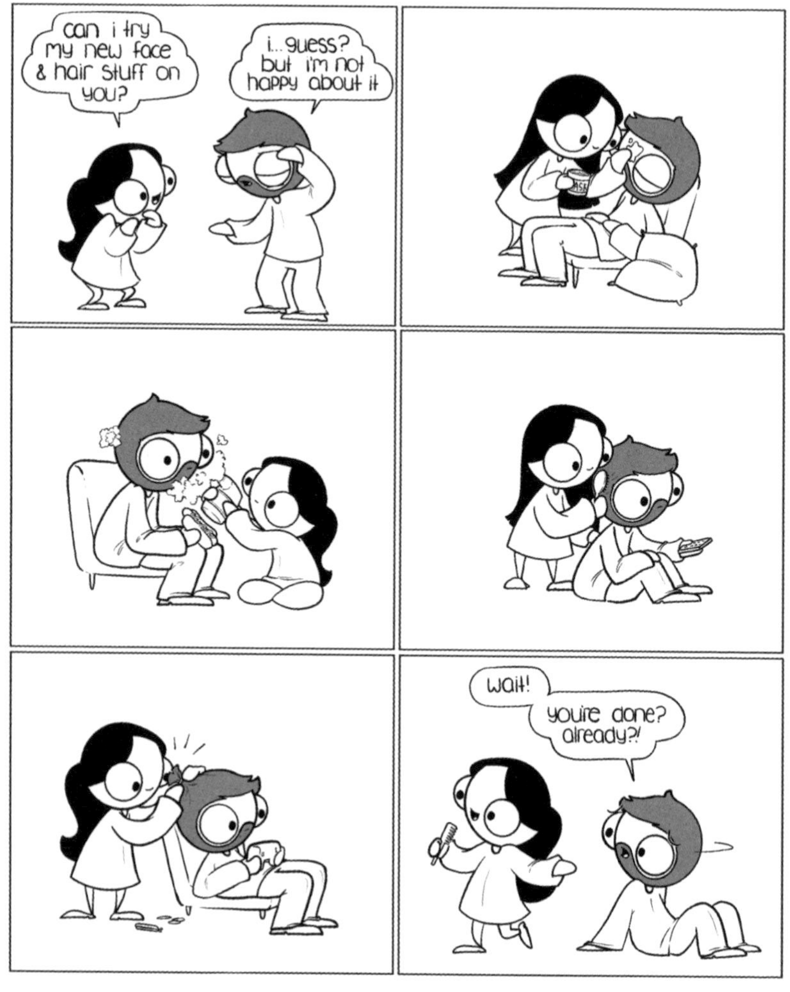
can i try my new face & hair stuff on you?
i...guess? but i'm not happy about it
wait!
you're done? already?!

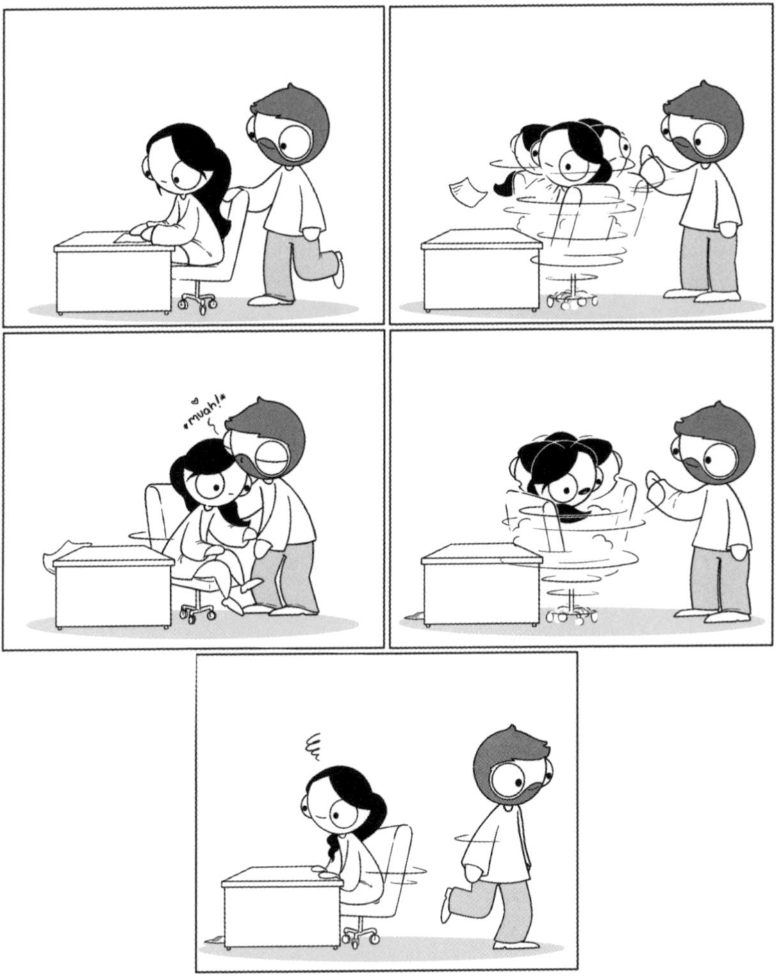
muah!

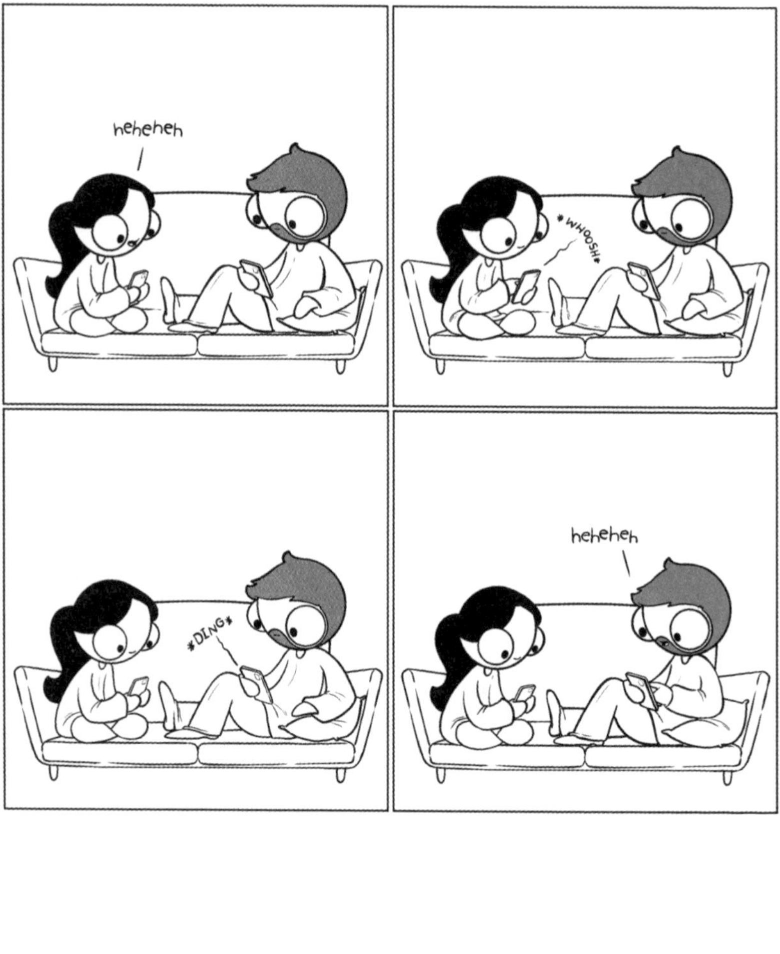
heheheh
WHOOSH
DING
heheheh

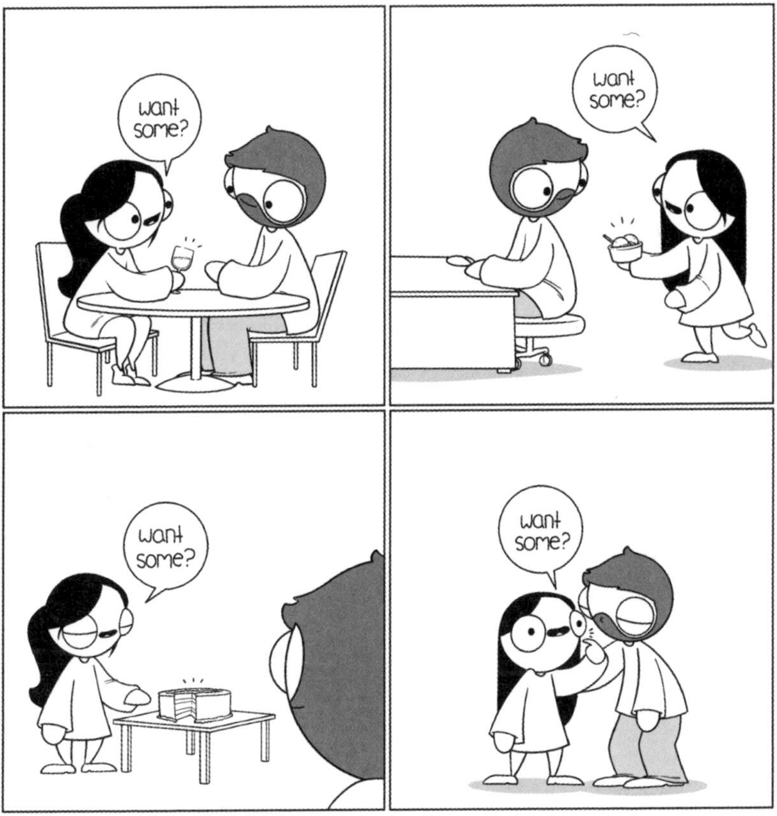
want some?
want some?
want some?
want some?

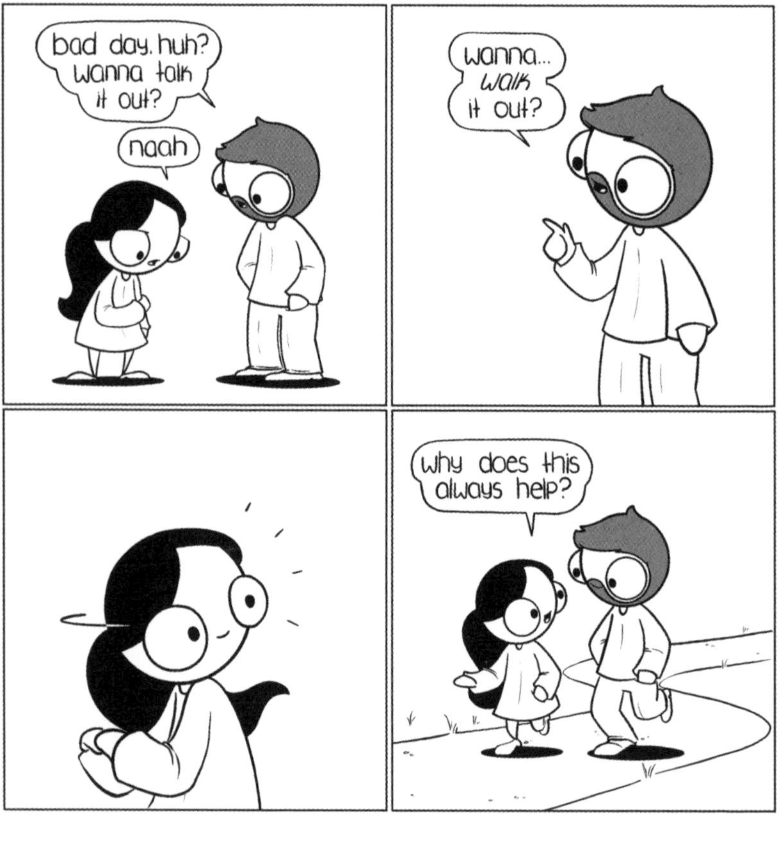
bad day. huh? wanna talk it out?
naah
wanna... *walk* it out?
why does this always help?

"cold hands"

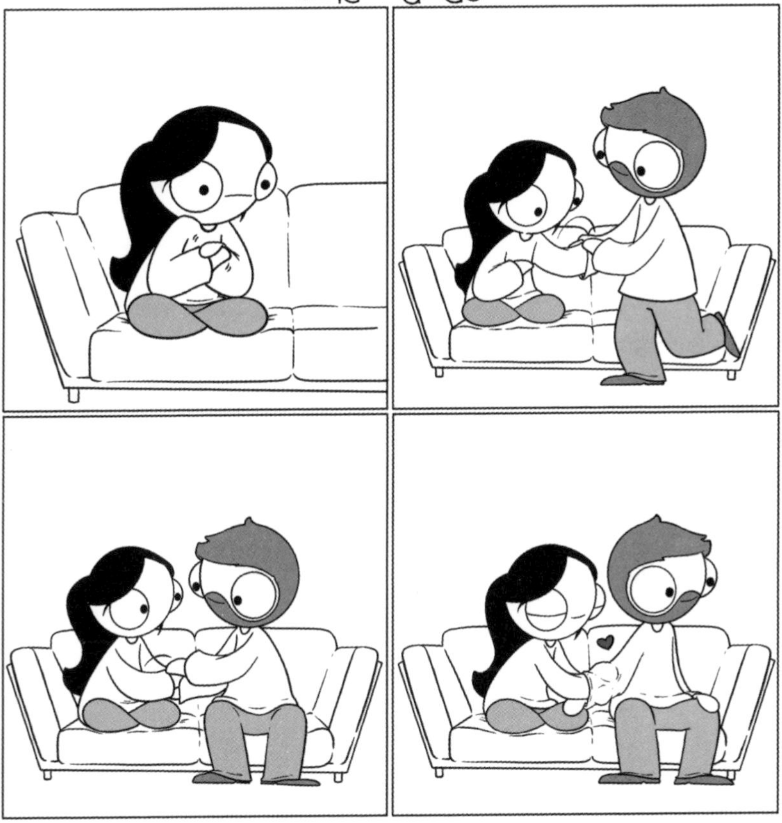

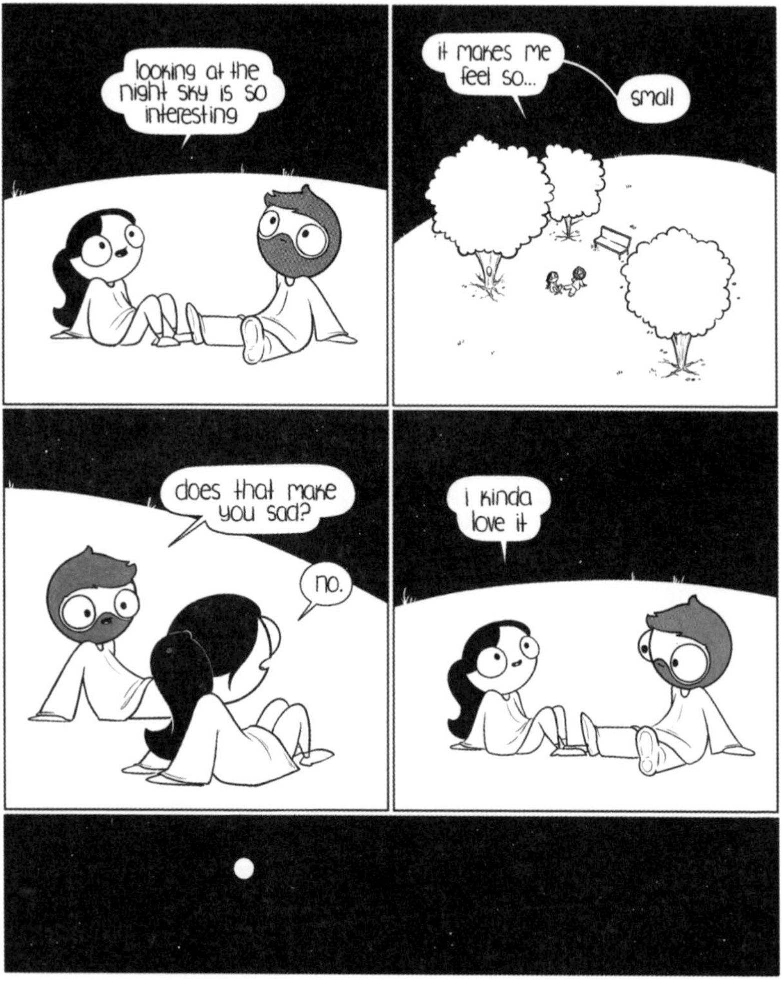
looking at the night sky is so interesting
it makes me feel so...
small
does that make you sad?
no.
i kinda love it

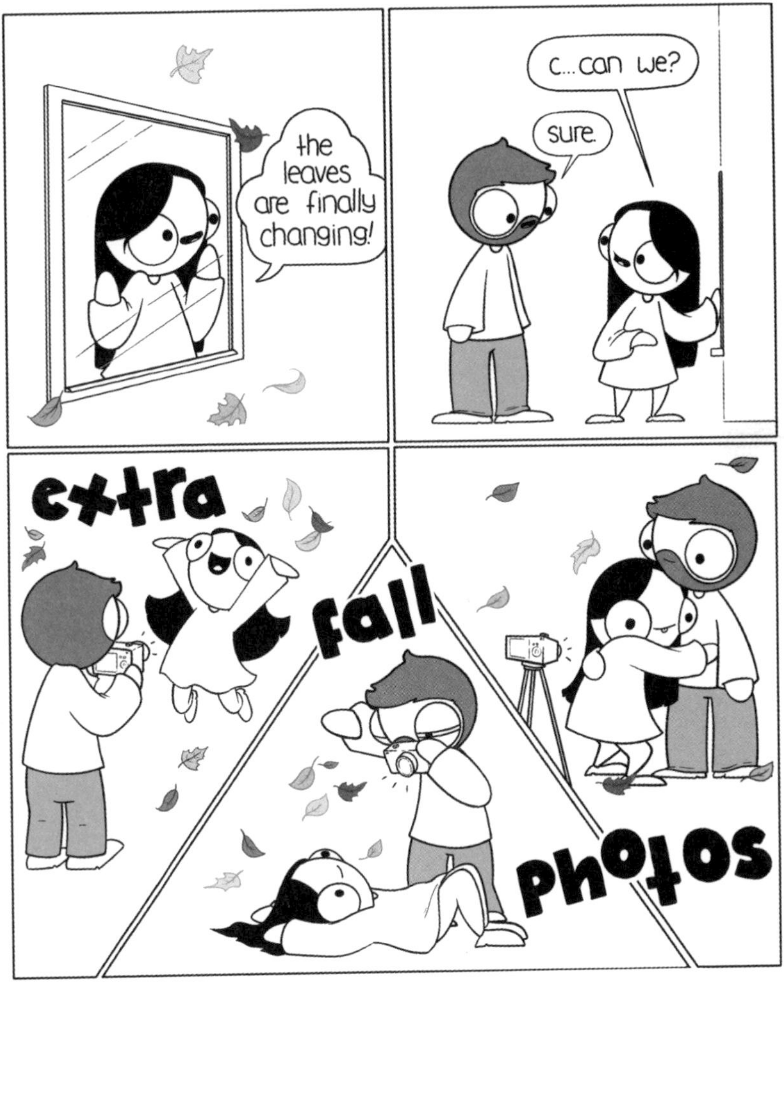

the leaves are finally changing!
c...can we?
sure.
extra
fall
photos

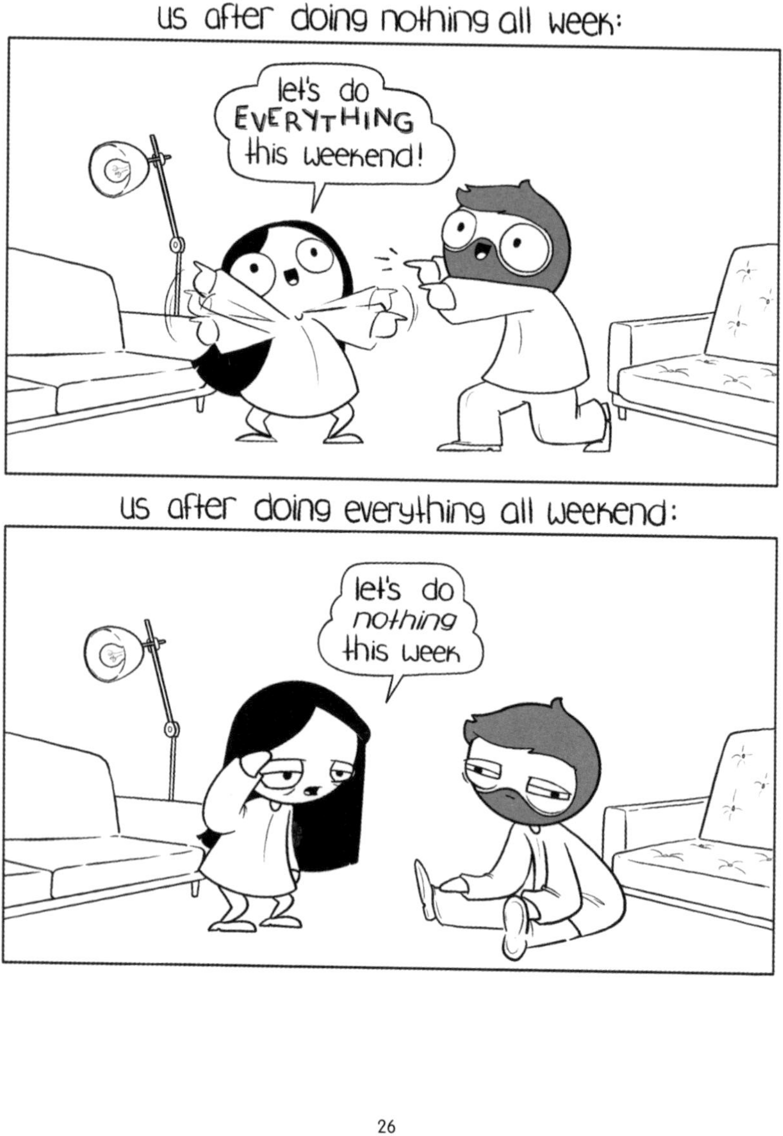
us after doing nothing all week:
let's do EVERYTHING this weekend!
us after doing everything all weekend:
let's do *nothing* this week

the Annual Winter Fuzz Increase

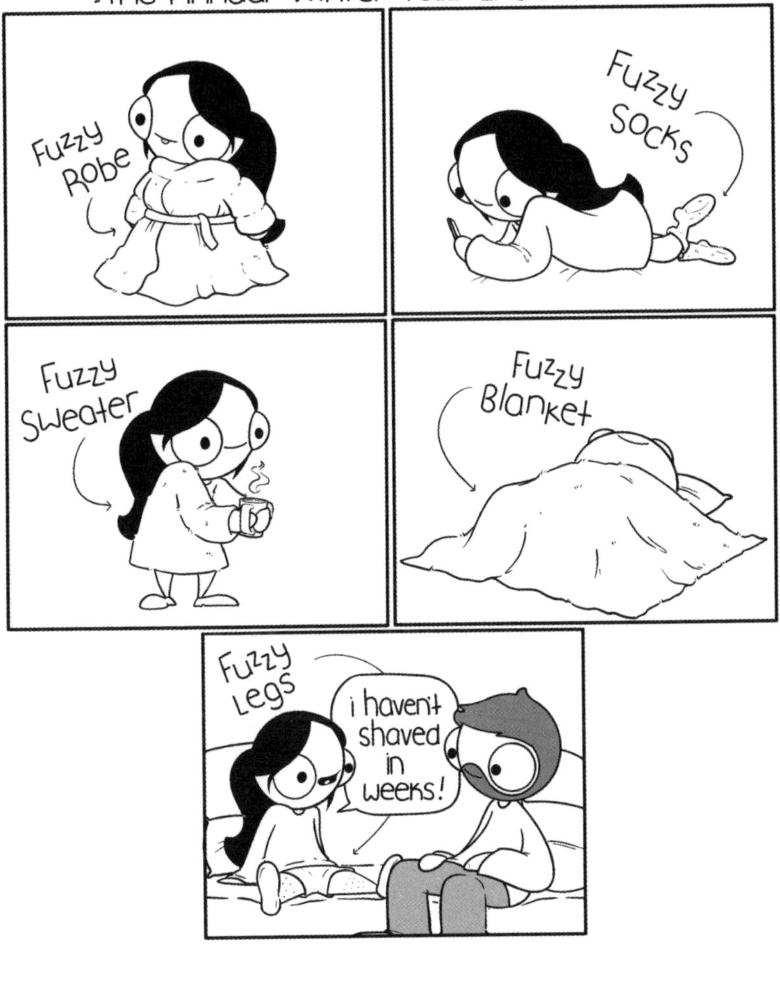

Fuzzy Robe
Fuzzy Socks
Fuzzy Sweater
Fuzzy Blanket
Fuzzy Legs
i haven't shaved in weeks!

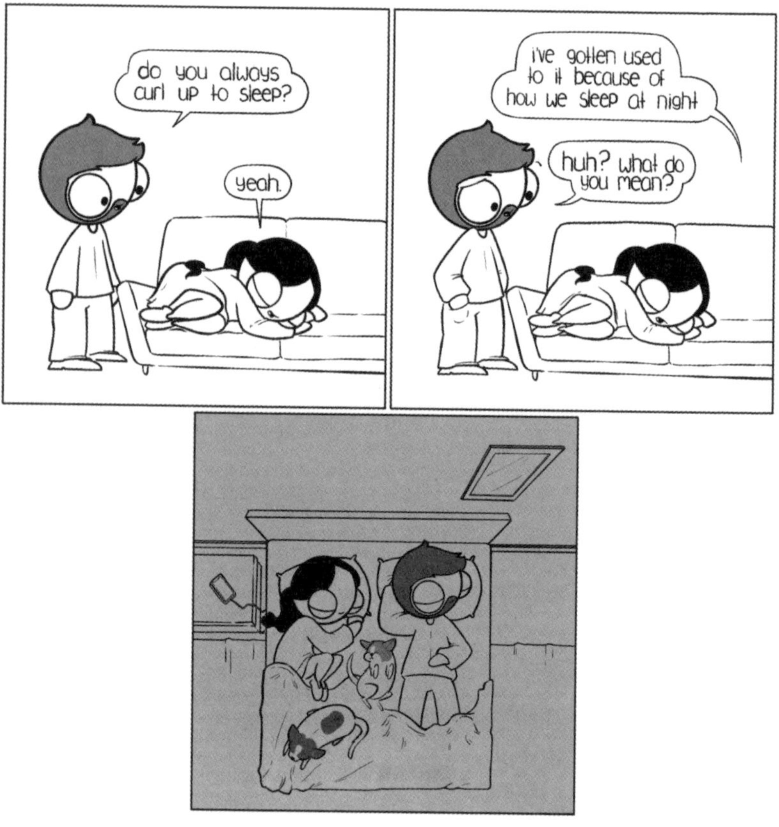
do you always curl up to sleep?
yeah.
i've gotten used to it because of how we sleep at night
huh? what do you mean?

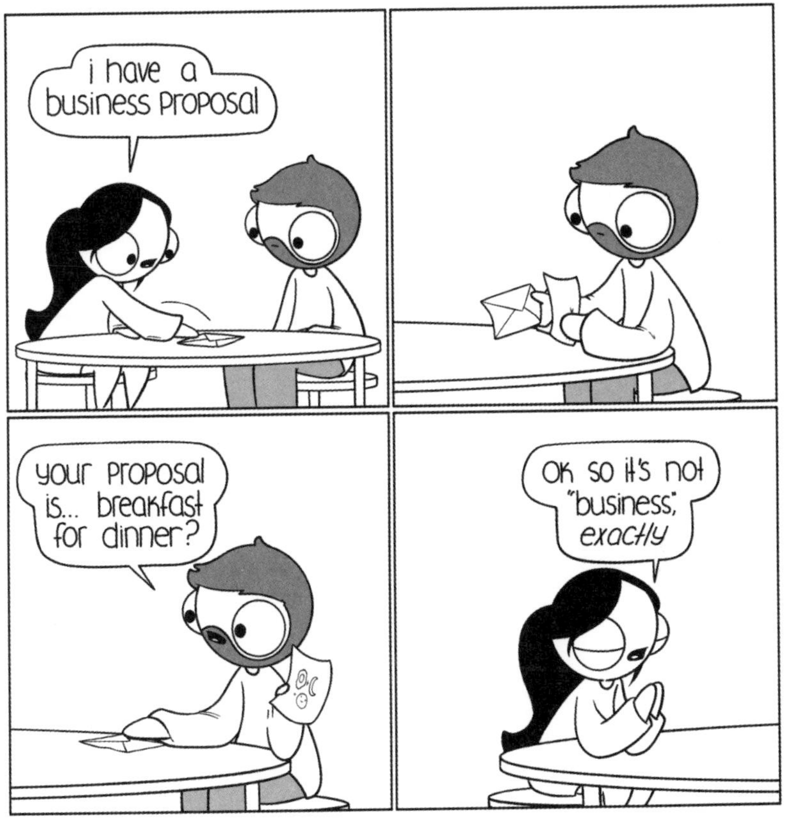
i have a business proposal
your proposal is... breakfast for dinner?
ok so it's not "business," *exactly*

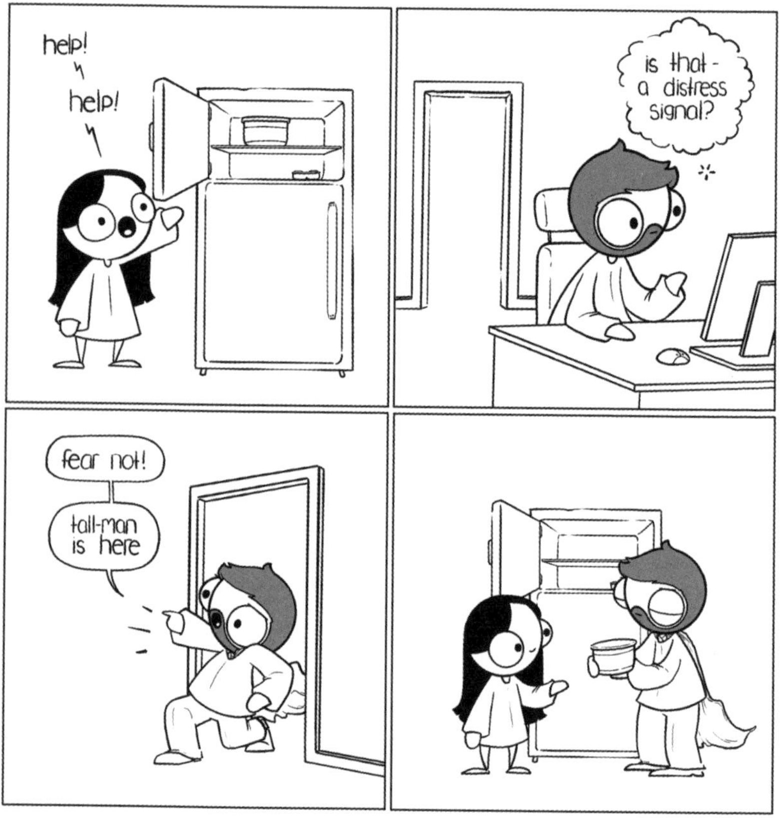
help!
help!
is that -
a distress
signal?
fear not!
tall-man
is here

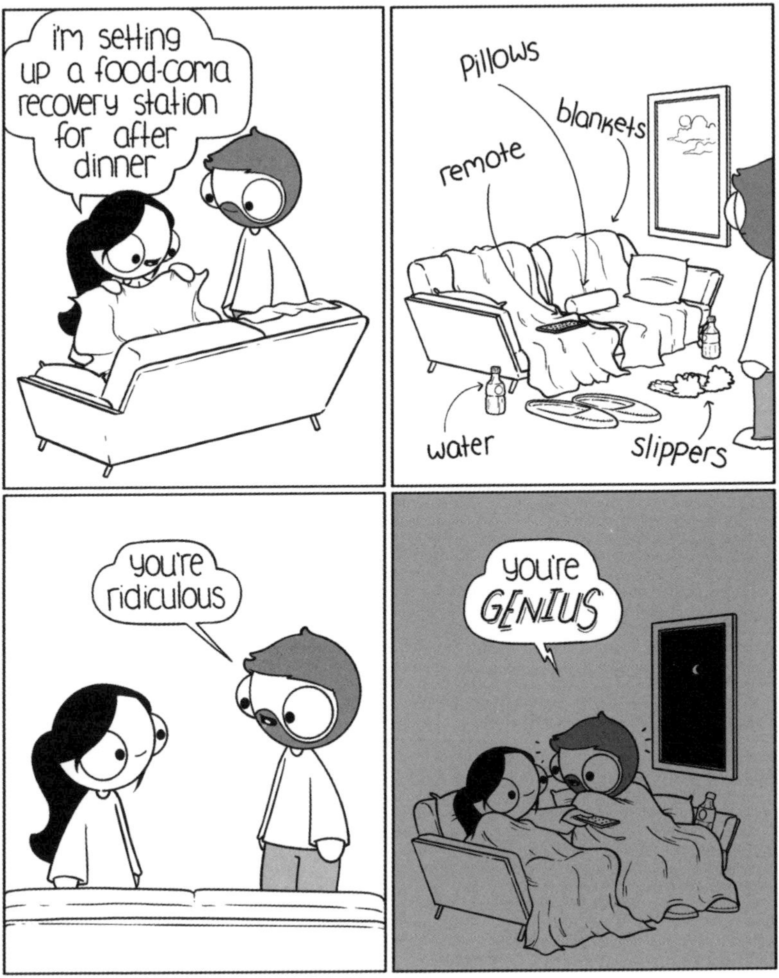
i'm setting up a food-coma recovery station for after dinner
pillows
blankets
remote
water
slippers
you're ridiculous
you're GENIUS

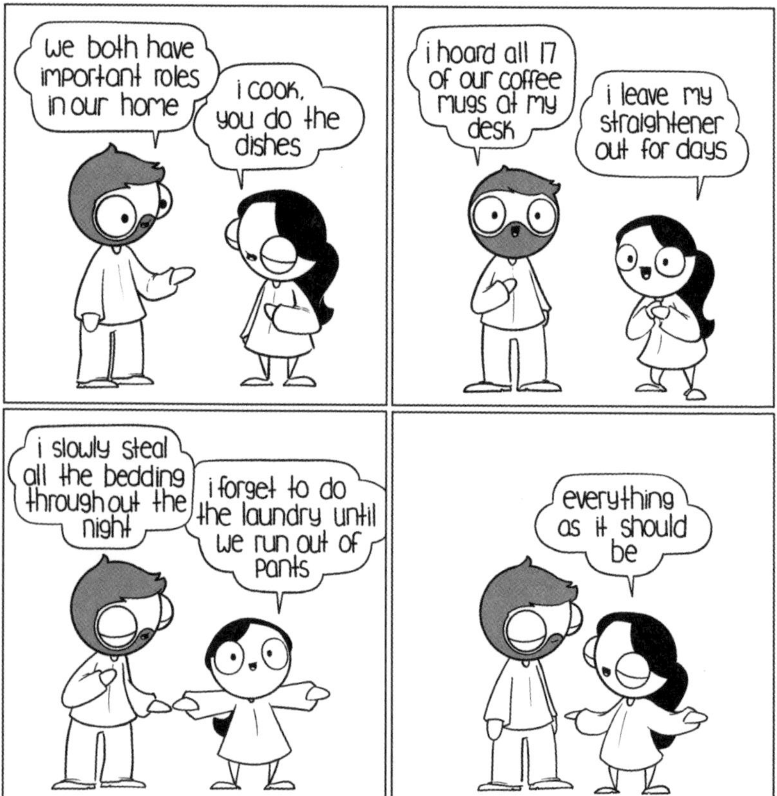
we both have important roles in our home
i cook, you do the dishes
i hoard all 17 of our coffee mugs at my desk
i leave my straightener out for days
i slowly steal all the bedding throughout the night
i forget to do the laundry until we run out of pants
everything as it should be

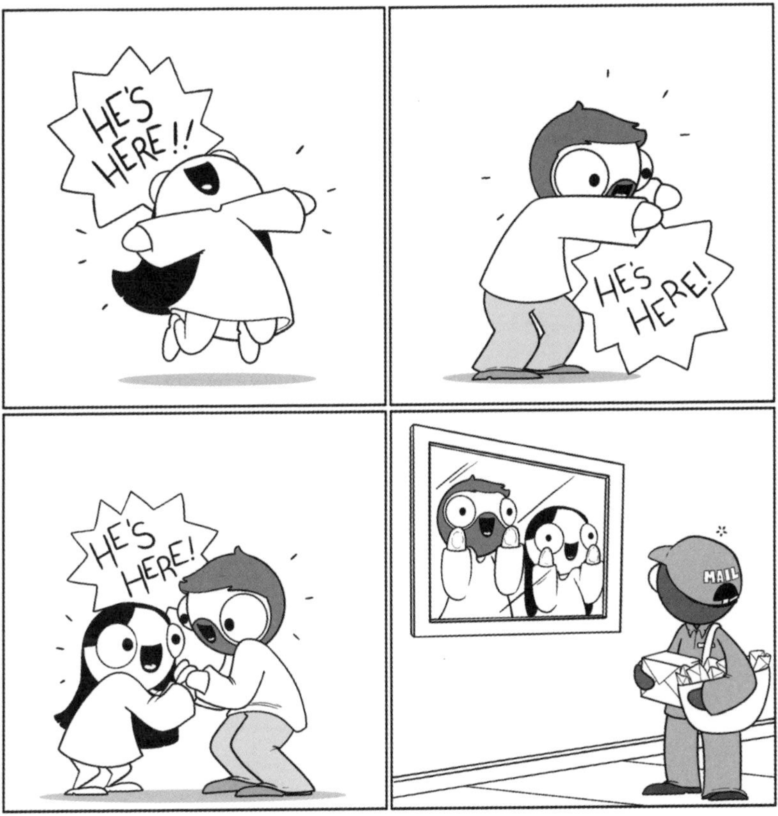
HE'S HERE!!
HE'S HERE!
HE'S HERE!
MAIL

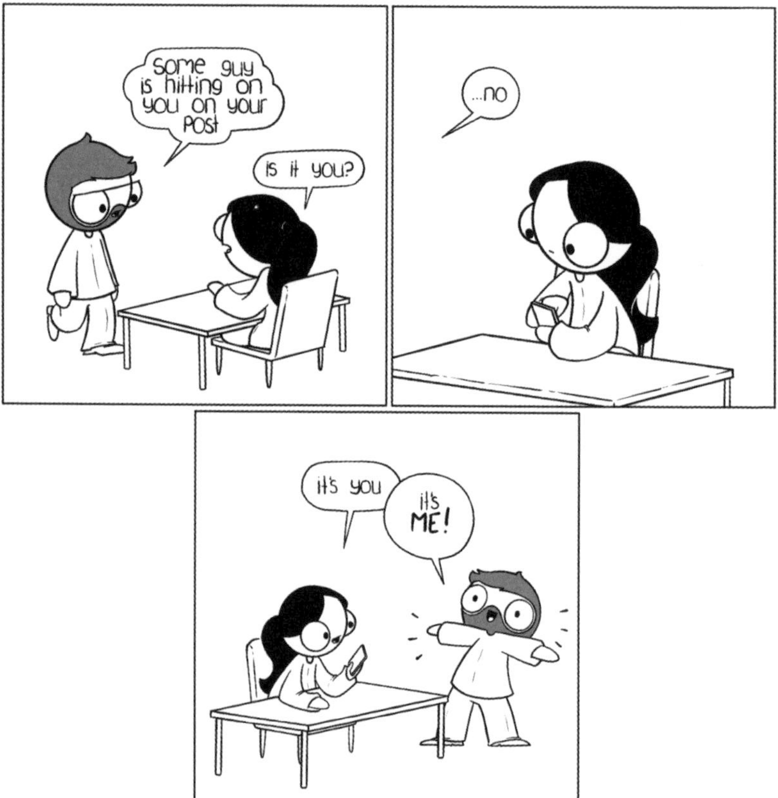
some guy is hitting on you on your post
is it you?
...no
it's you
it's ME!

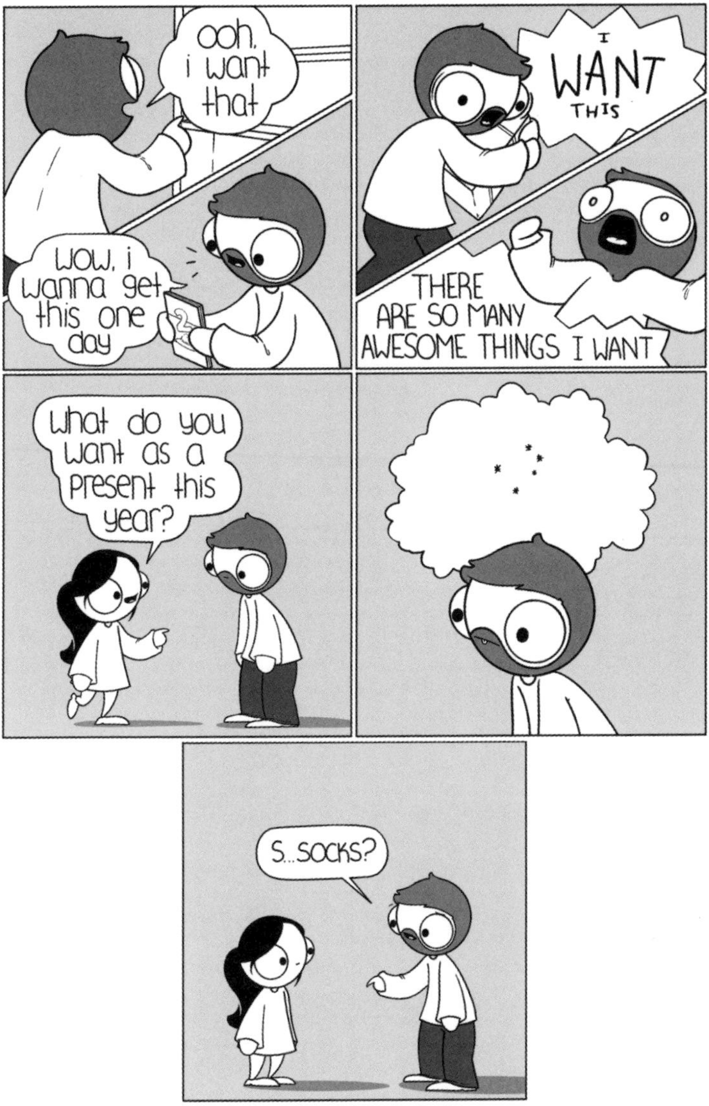
ooh. i want that
wow, i wanna get this one day
I WANT THIS
THERE ARE SO MANY AWESOME THINGS I WANT
What do you want as a present this year?
S...SOCKS?

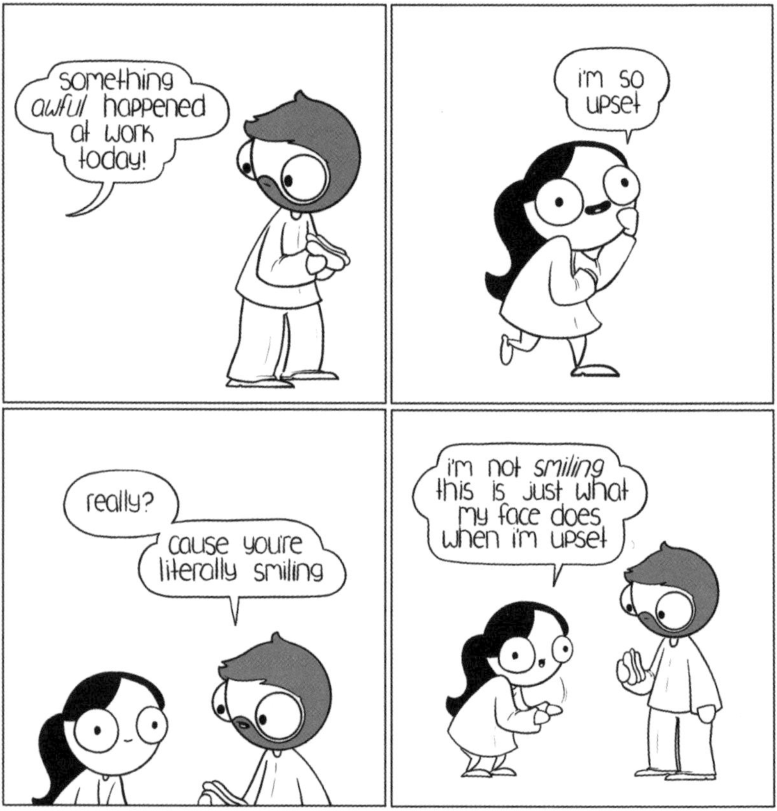
something *awful* happened at work today!
i'm so upset
really?
cause you're literally smiling
i'm not *smiling* this is just what my face does when i'm upset

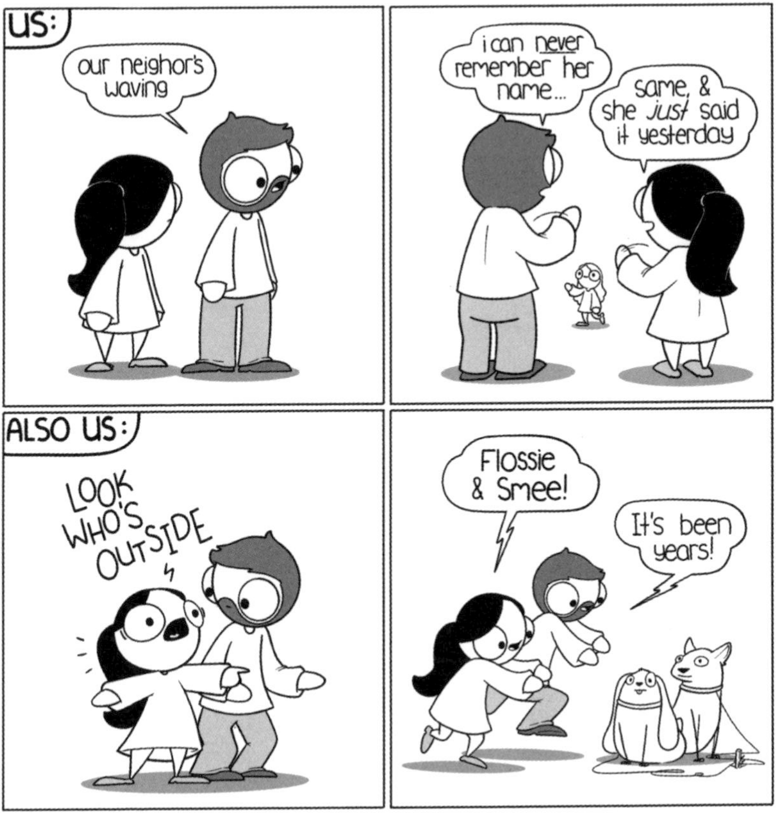
US:
our neighor's waving
i can never remember her name...
same, & she just said it yesterday
ALSO US:
LOOK WHO'S OUTSIDE
Flossie & Smee!
It's been years!

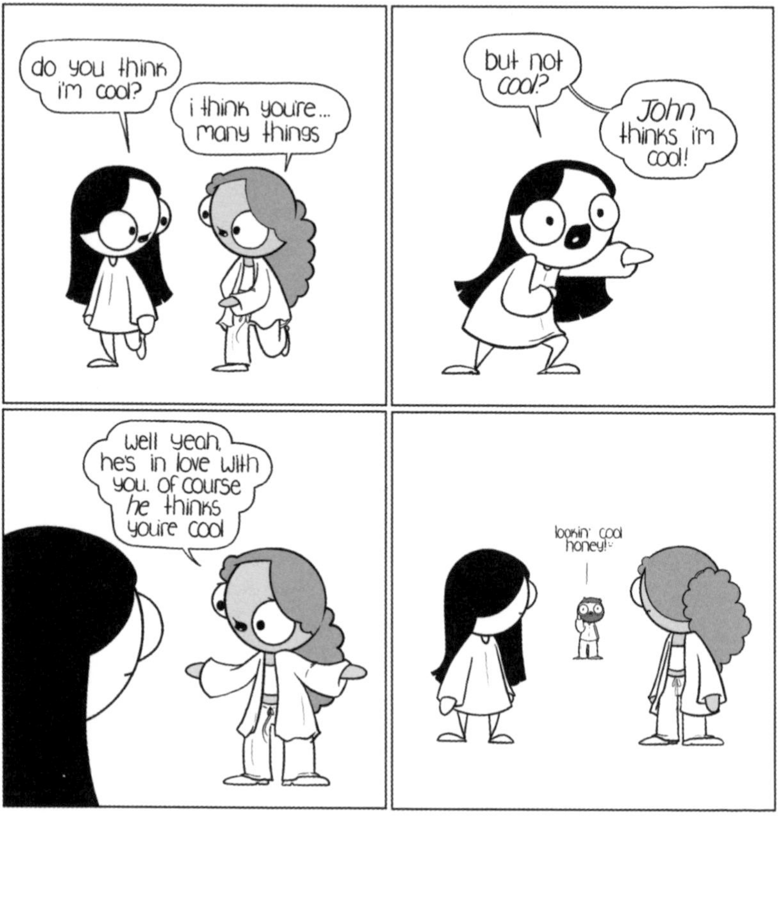
do you think i'm cool?
i think you're... many things
but not *cool?*
John thinks i'm cool!
well yeah, he's in love with you. of course *he* thinks you're cool
lookin' cool honey!

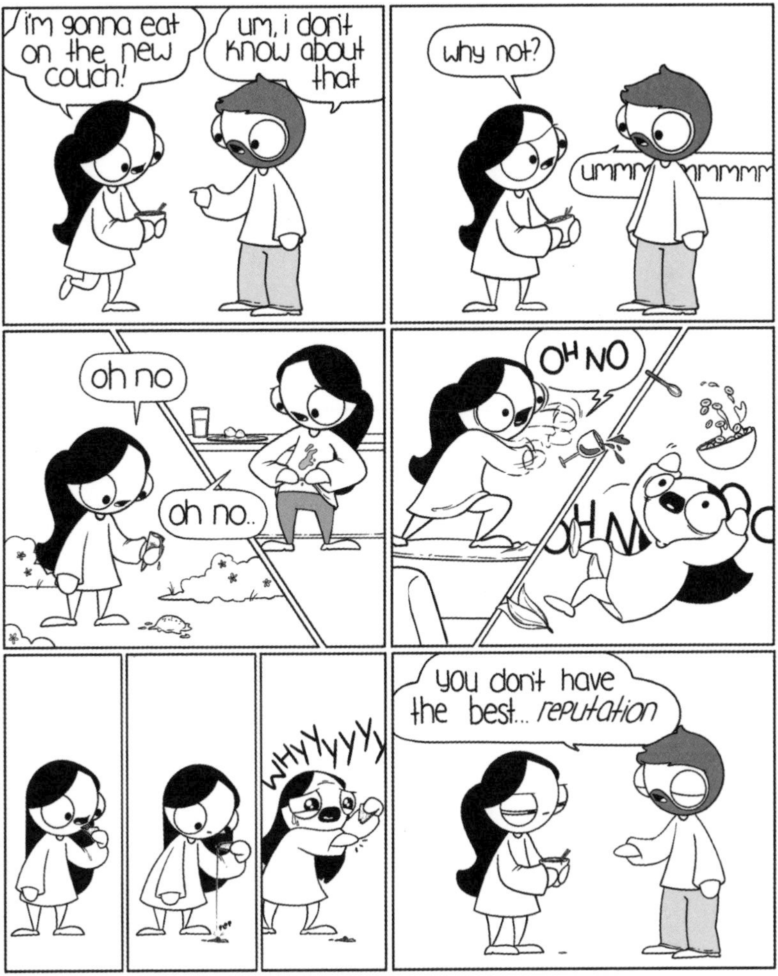
i'm gonna eat on the new couch!
um, i don't know about that
why not?
ummmmmmmm
oh no
oh no..
OH NO
OH NOOO
WHYYyyyYy
you don't have the best... *reputation*

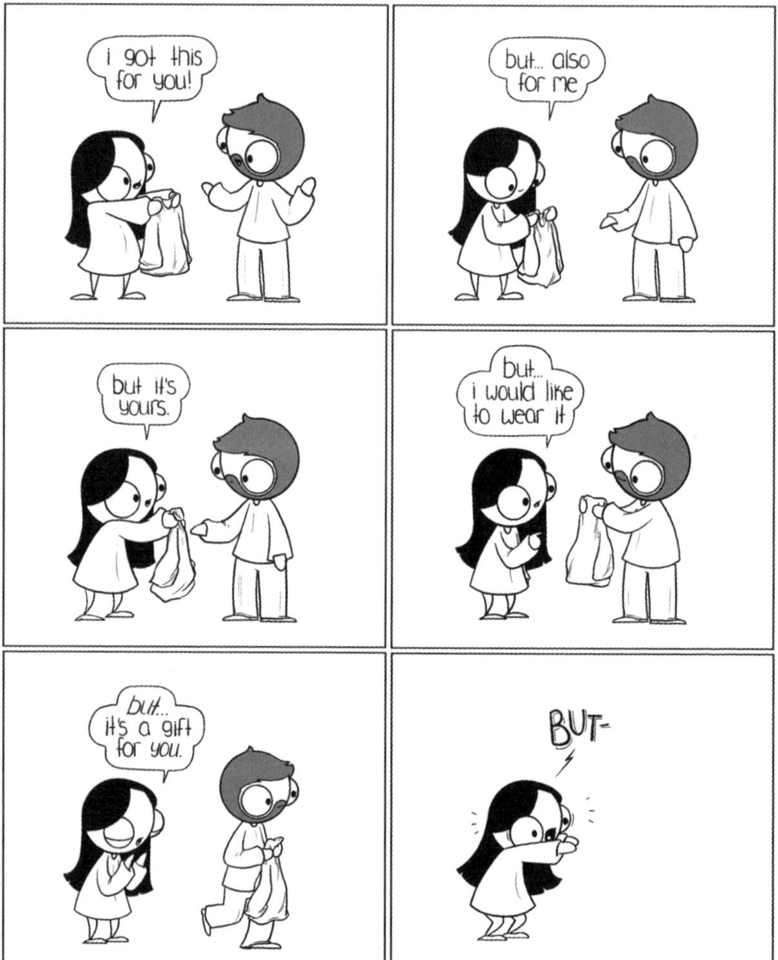
i got this for you!
but... also for me
but it's yours.
but... i would like to wear it
but... it's a gift for you.
BUT-

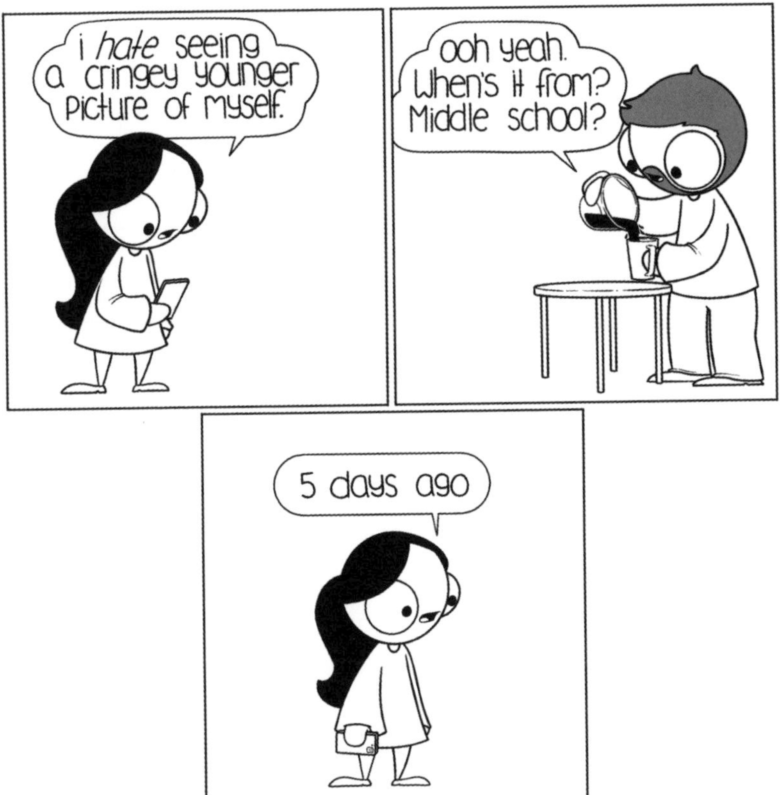
i *hate* seeing a cringey younger picture of myself.
ooh yeah. When's it from? Middle school?
5 days ago

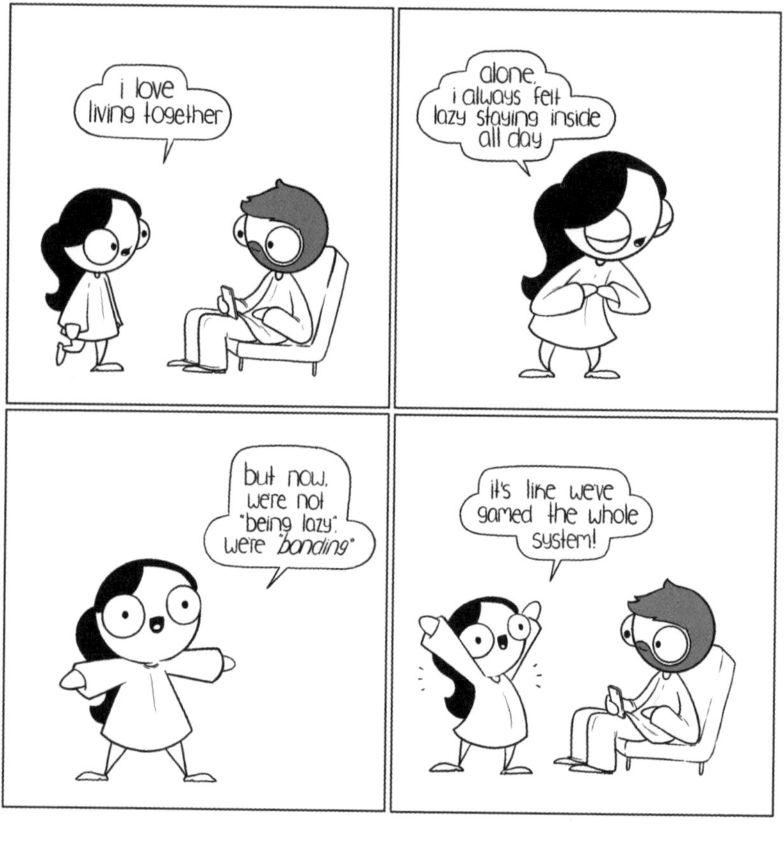
i love living together
alone, i always felt lazy staying inside all day
but now, we're not "being lazy", we're "bonding"
it's like we've gamed the whole system!

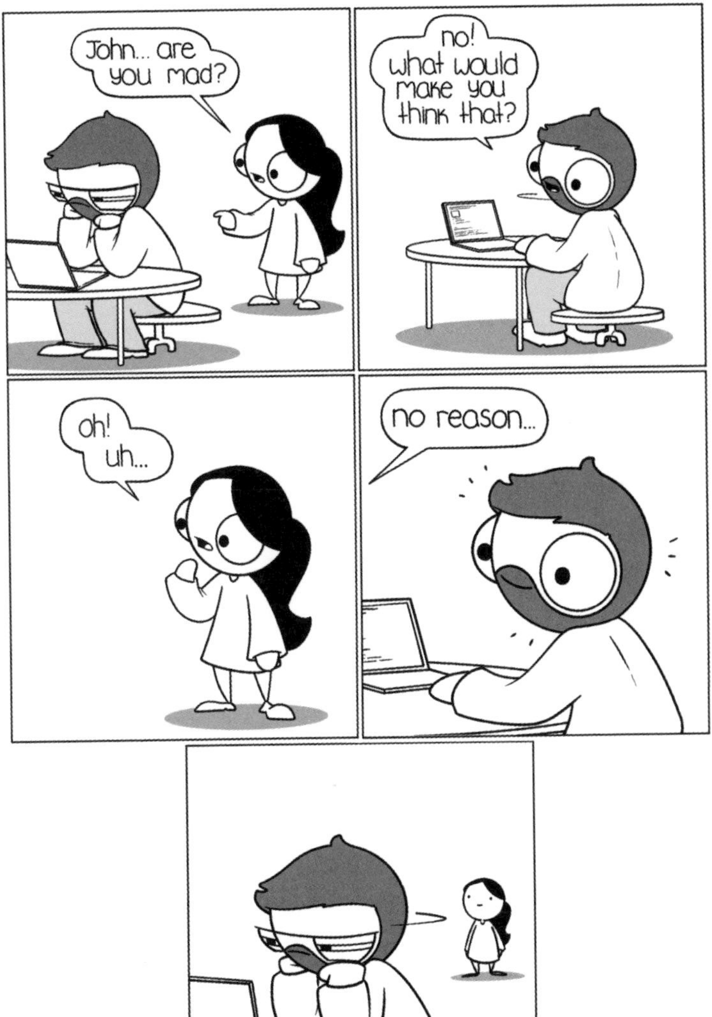
John... are you mad?
no! what would make you think that?
oh! uh...
no reason...

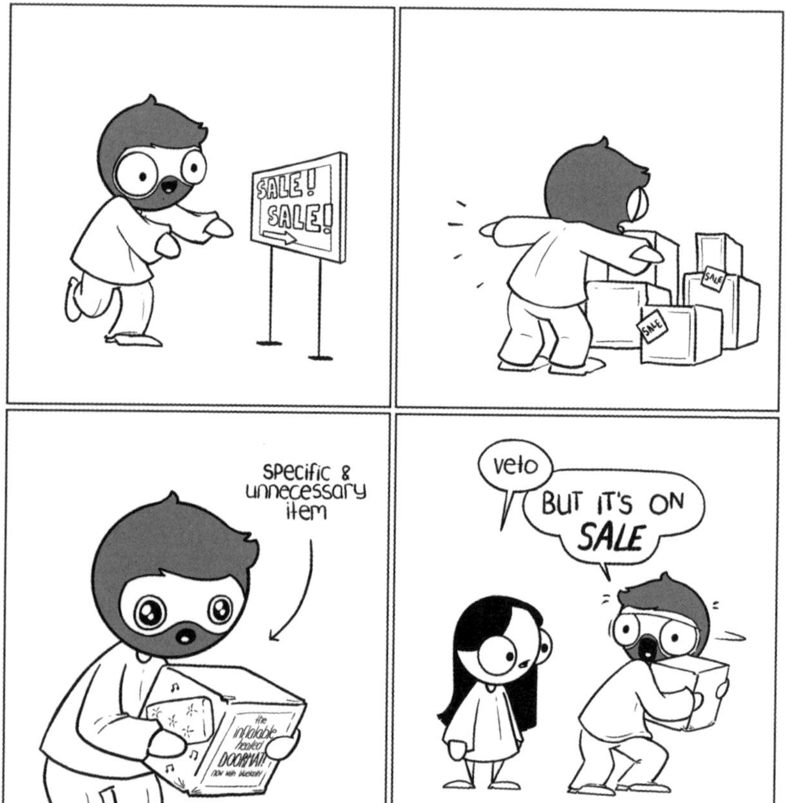
SALE!
SALE!
SALE
SALE
specific &
unnecessary
item
the
inflatable
heated
DOORMAT!
now with bluetooth
veto
BUT IT'S ON
SALE

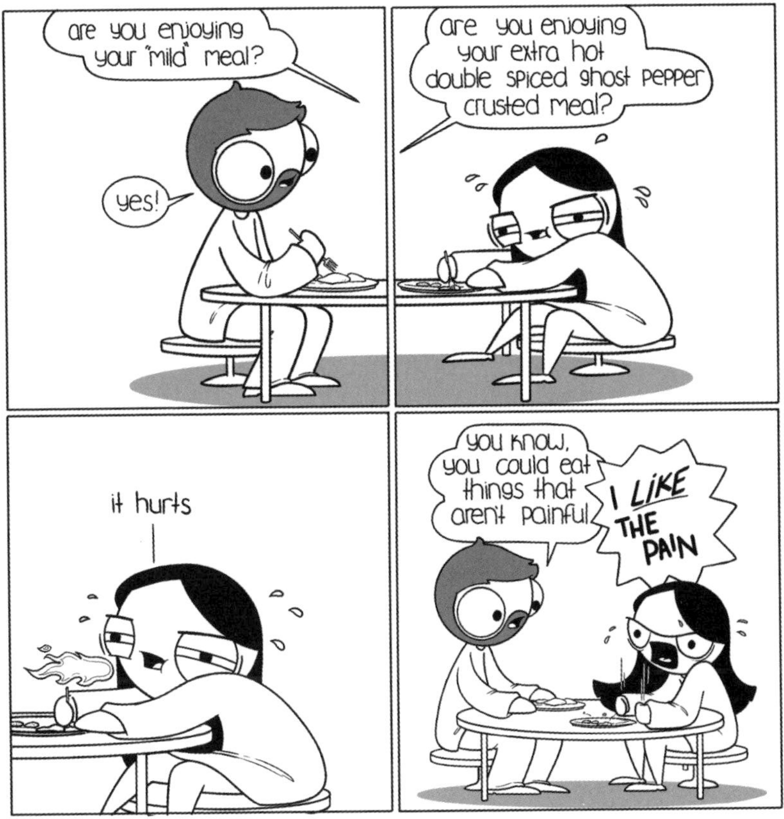
are you enjoying your "mild" meal?
yes!
are you enjoying your extra hot double spiced ghost pepper crusted meal?
it hurts
you know, you could eat things that aren't painful
I LIKE THE PAIN

when you cook a new recipe

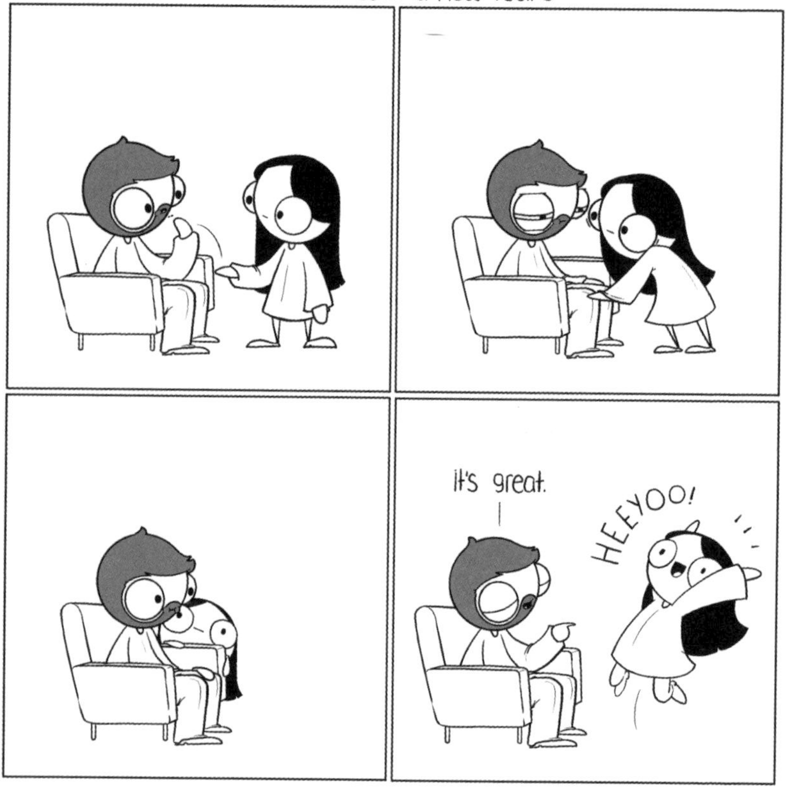
it's great.
HEEYOO!

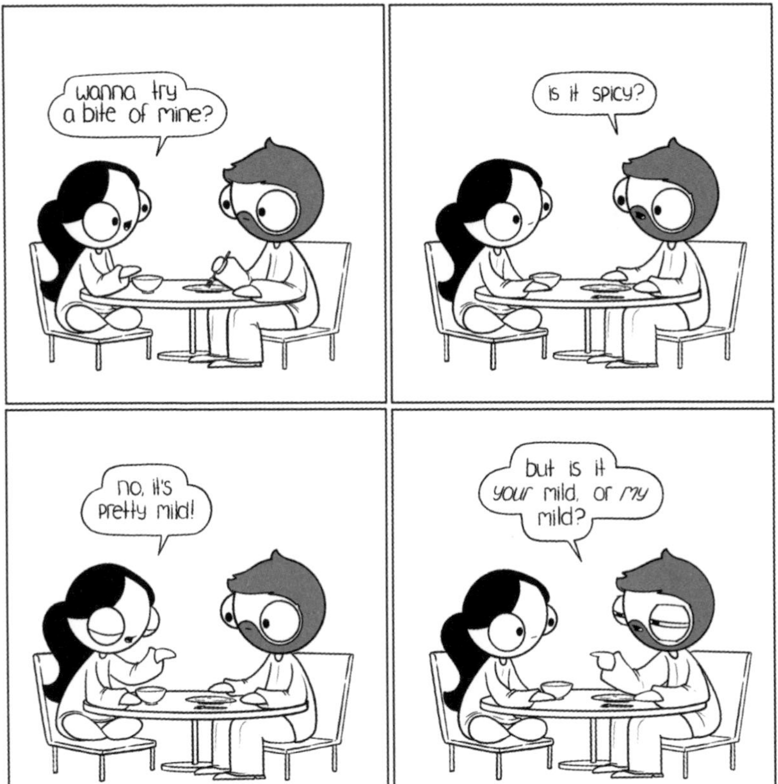
wanna try a bite of mine?
is it spicy?
no, it's pretty mild!
but is it *your* mild, or *my* mild?

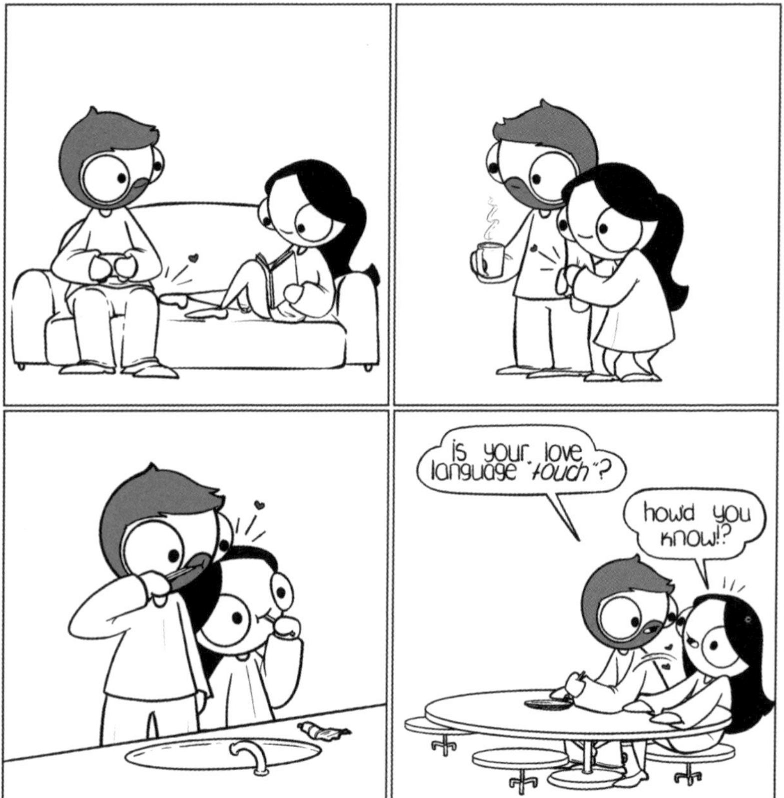
is your love language "touch"?
how'd you know!?

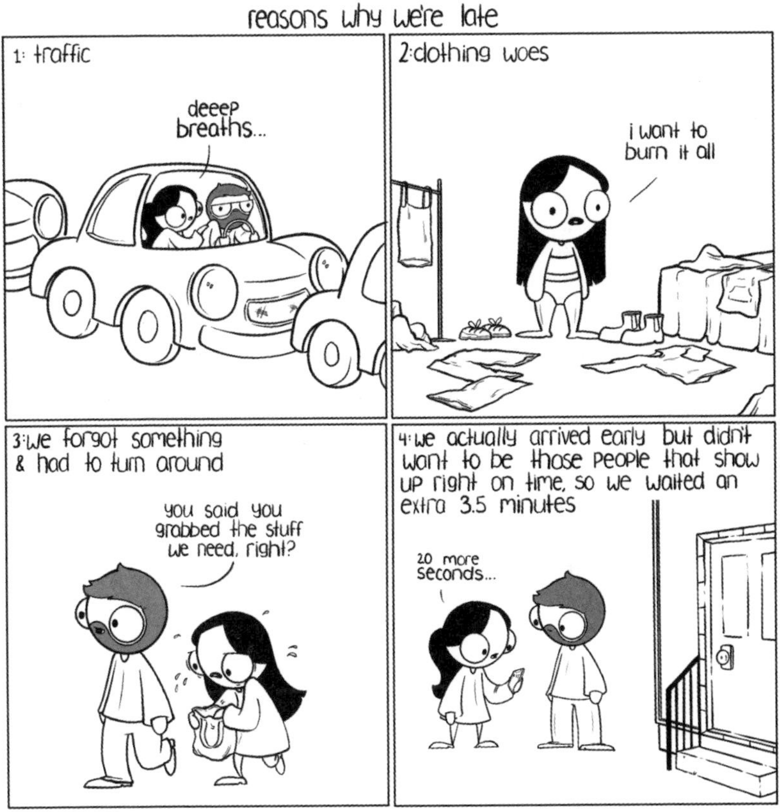
reasons why we're late
1: traffic
deeep breaths...
2:clothing woes
i want to burn it all
3:we forgot something & had to turn around
you said you grabbed the stuff we need, right?
4:we actually arrived early but didn't want to be those people that show up right on time, so we waited an extra 3.5 minutes
20 more seconds...

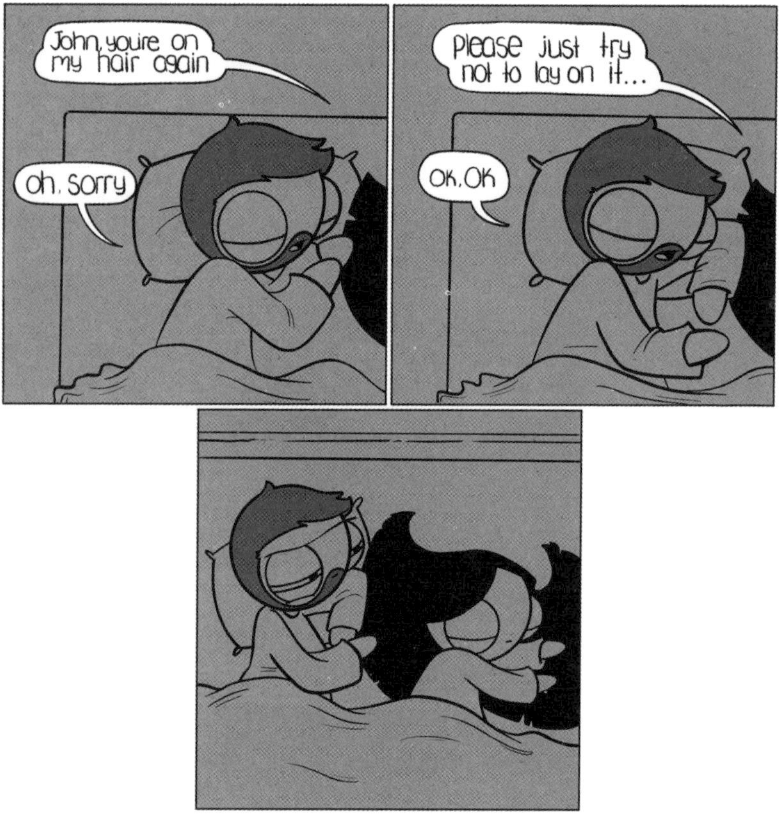
John, youre on my hair again
oh. sorry
Please just try not to lay on it...
OK, OK

social battery

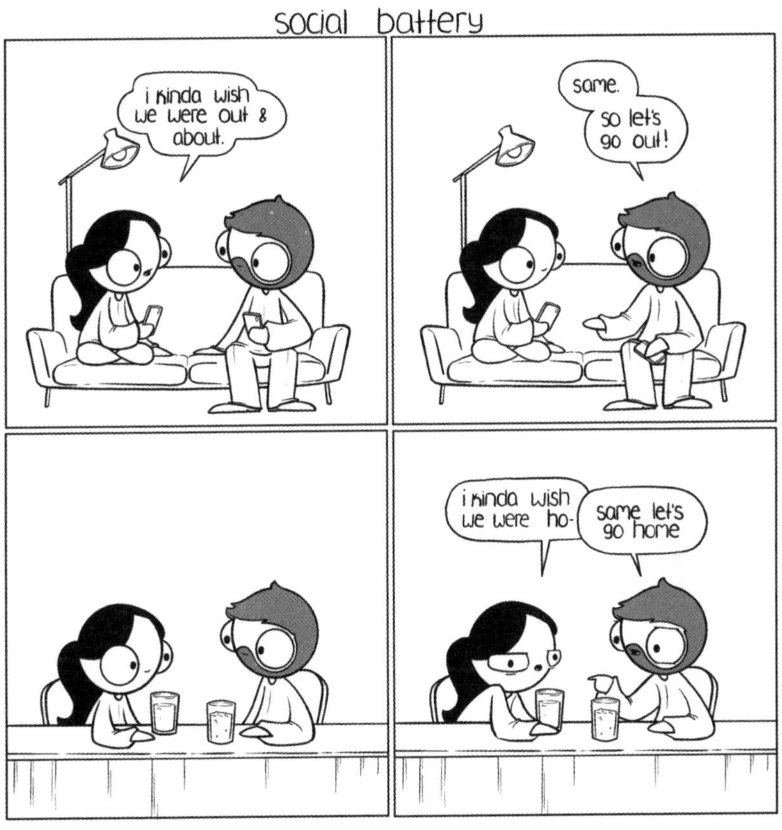
i kinda wish we were out & about.
same.
so let's go out!
i kinda wish we were ho-
same let's go home

the kind of artist i want to be:
Always working
constantly inspired
the kind of artist i am:
what should i draw what should i draw what should i draw what sho

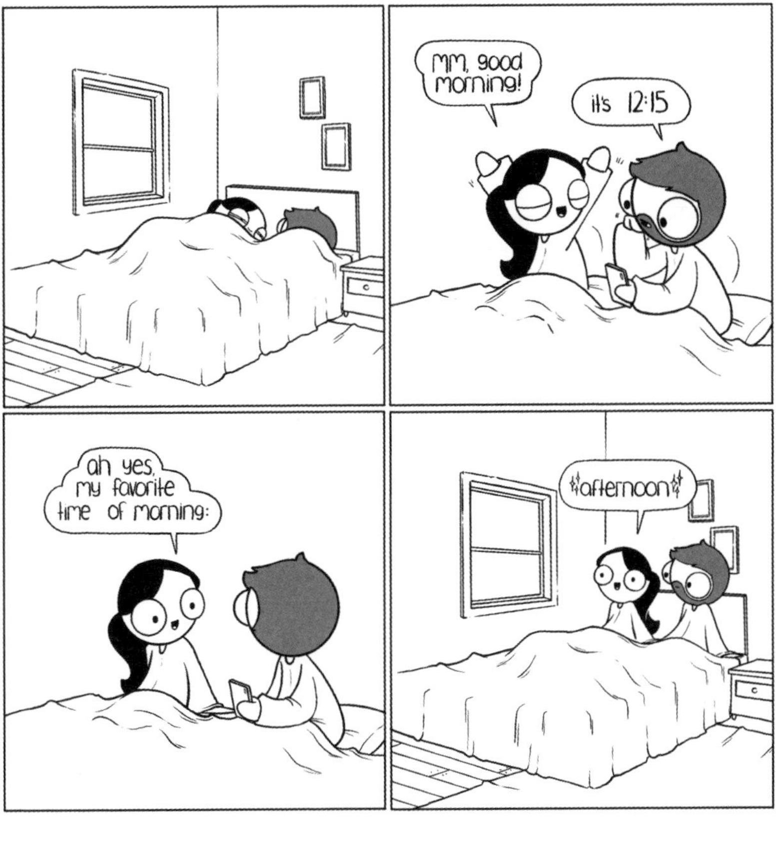
mm, good morning!
it's 12:15
ah yes, my favorite time of morning:
afternoon

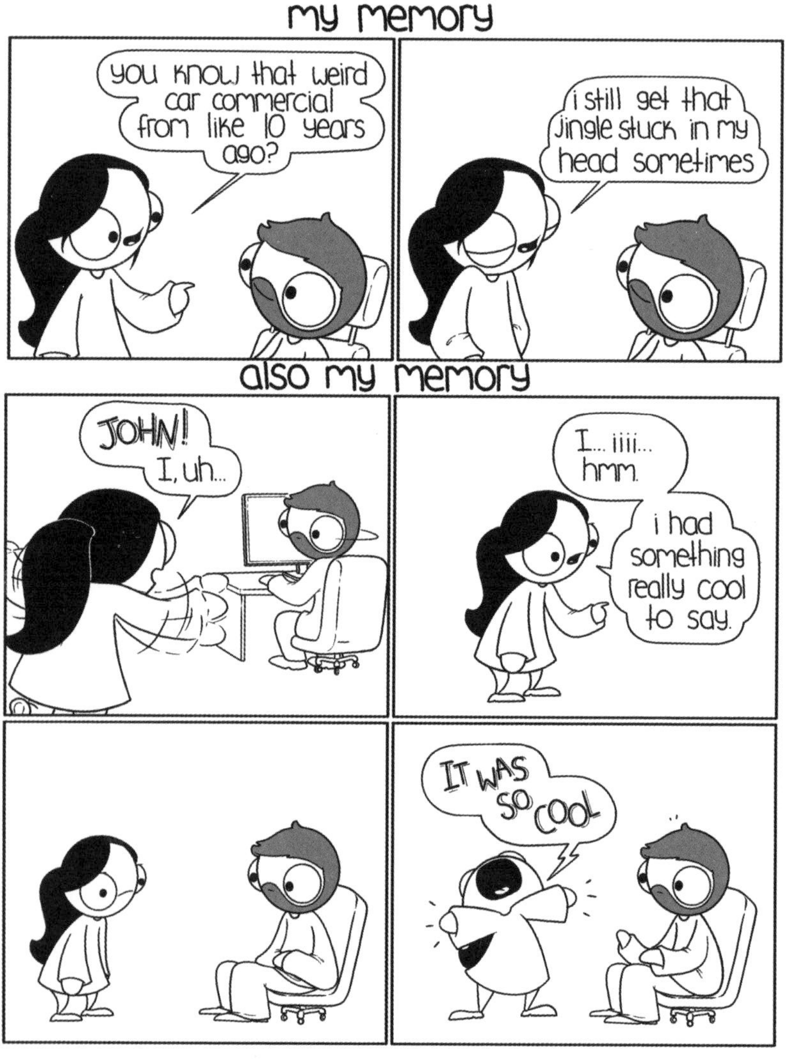
my memory
you know that weird car commercial from like 10 years ago?
i still get that jingle stuck in my head sometimes
also my memory
JOHN! I, uh...
I... iiii... hmm.
i had something really cool to say.
IT WAS SO COOL

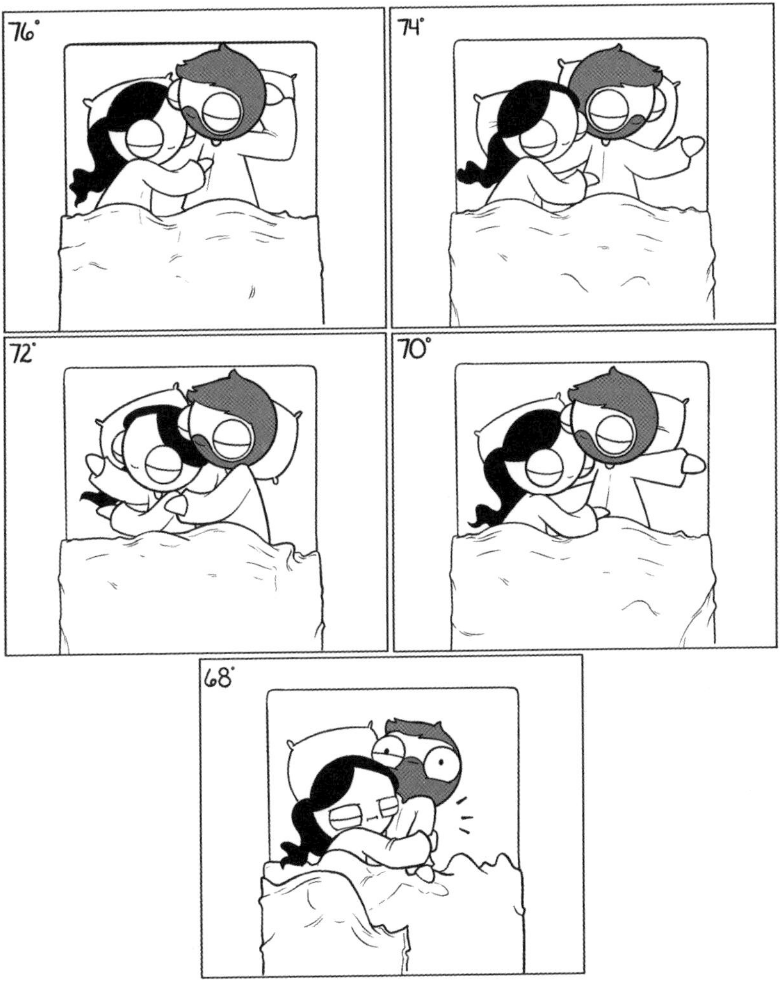
76°
74°
72°
70°
68°

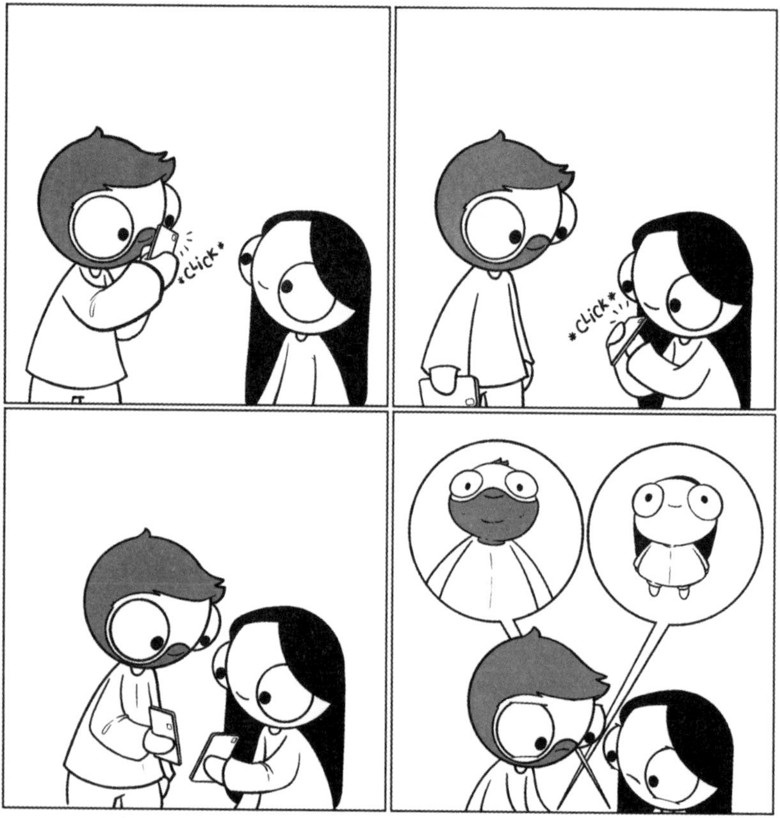
CLICK
CLICK

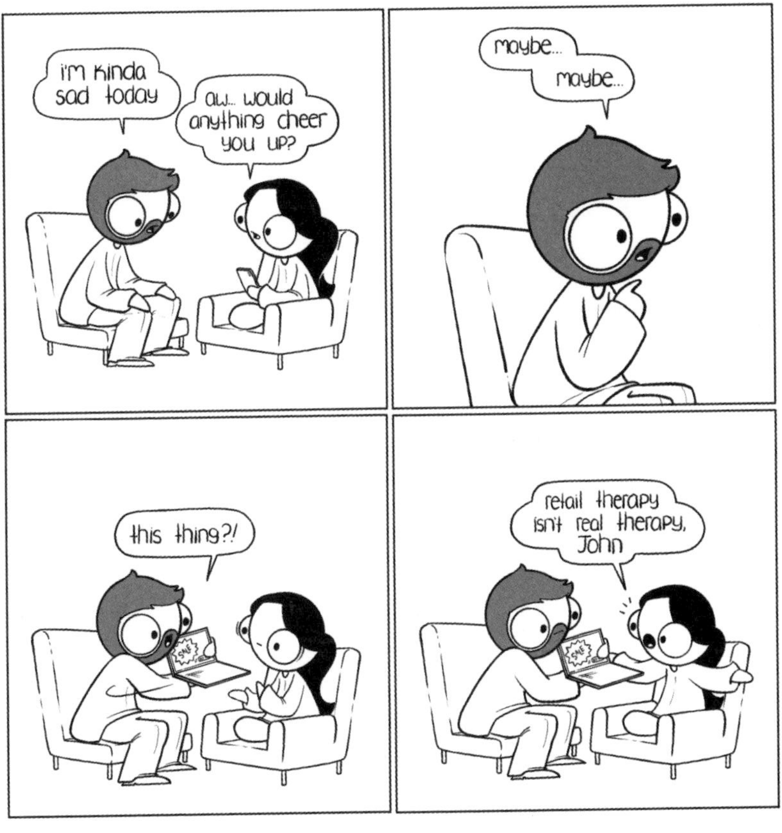
i'm kinda sad today
aw... would anything cheer you up?
maybe...
maybe...
this thing?!
retail therapy isn't real therapy, John

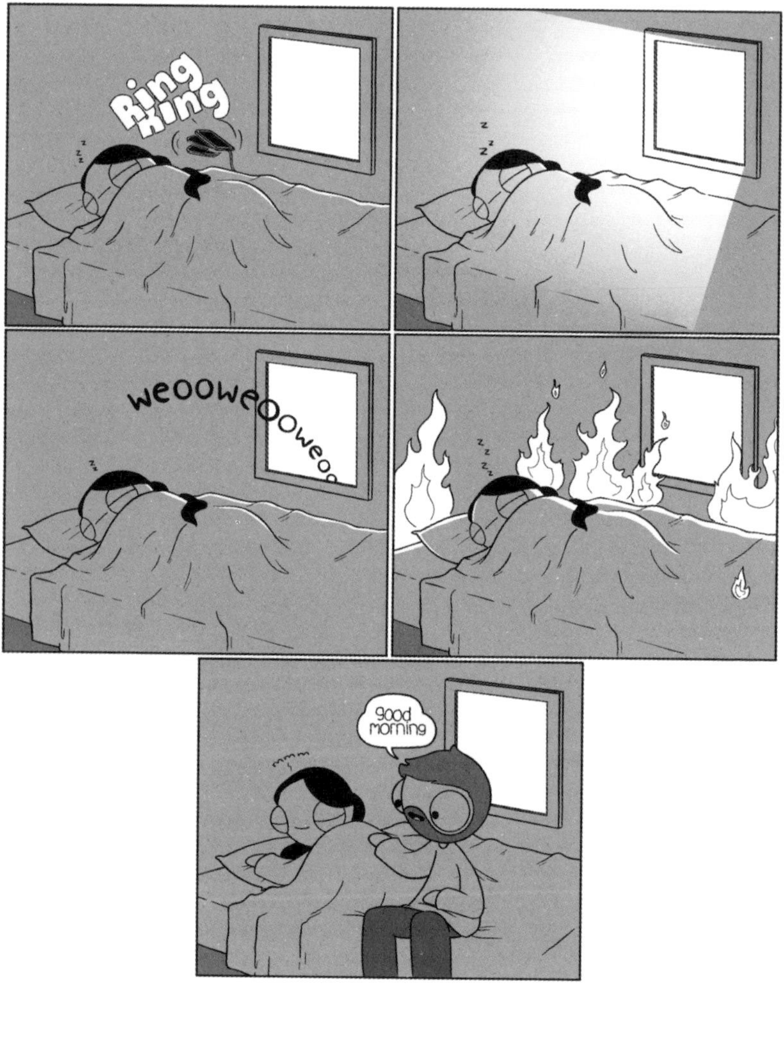
Ring Ring
weooweoOoweo
mmm
good morning

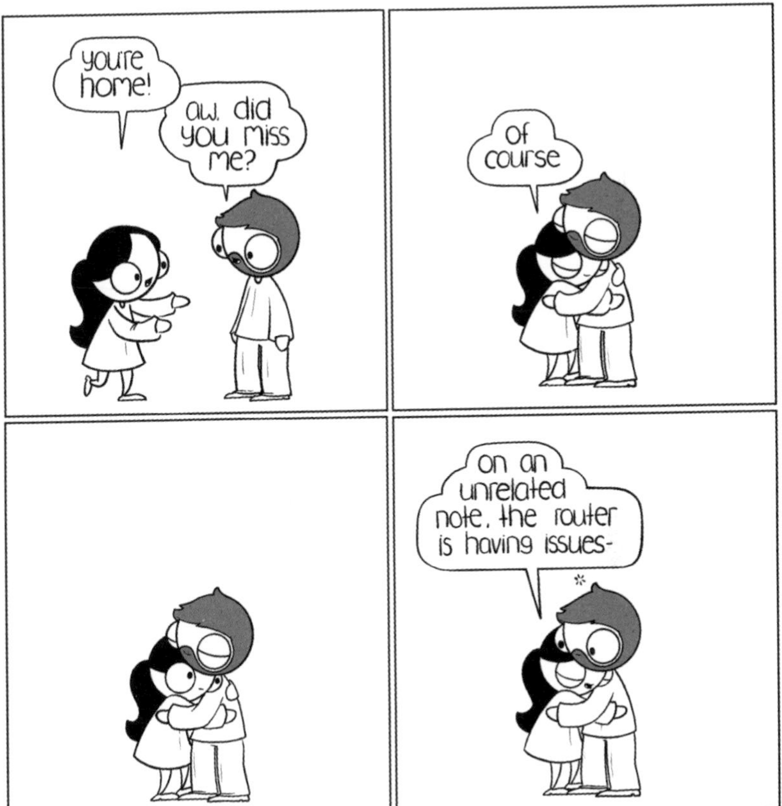
you're home!
aw, did you miss me?
of course
on an unrelated note, the router is having issues-

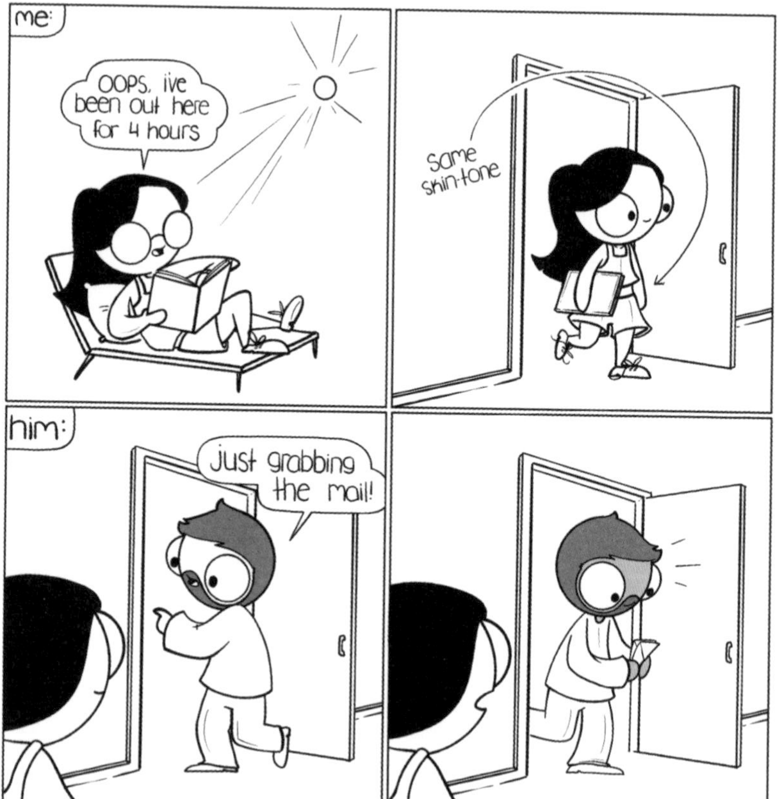
me:
OOPS, ive been out here for 4 hours
same skin-tone
him:
just grabbing the mail!

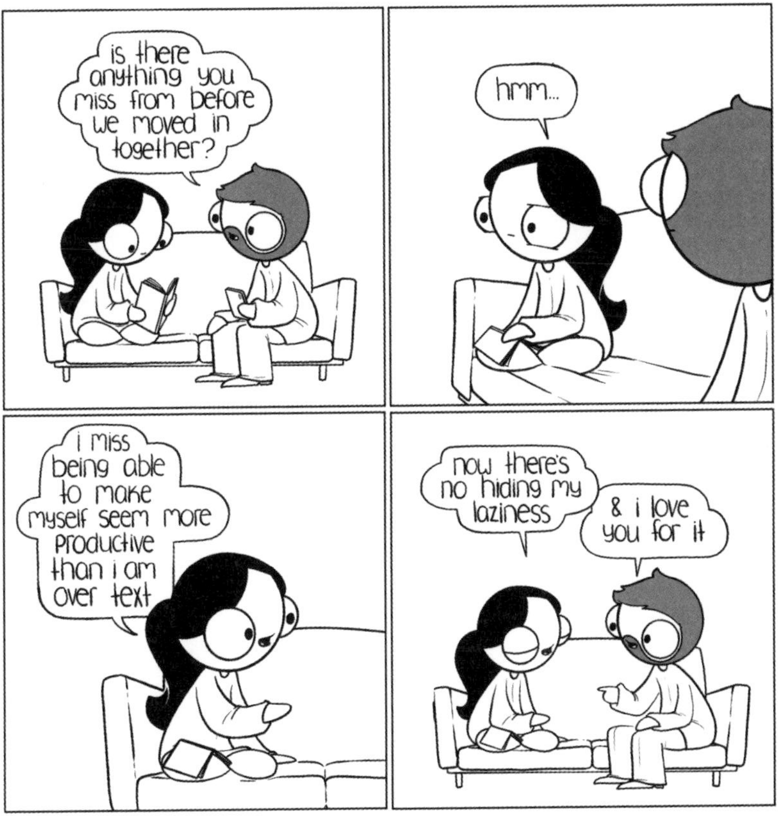
is there anything you miss from before we moved in together?
hmm...
i miss being able to make myself seem more productive than i am over text
now there's no hiding my laziness
& i love you for it

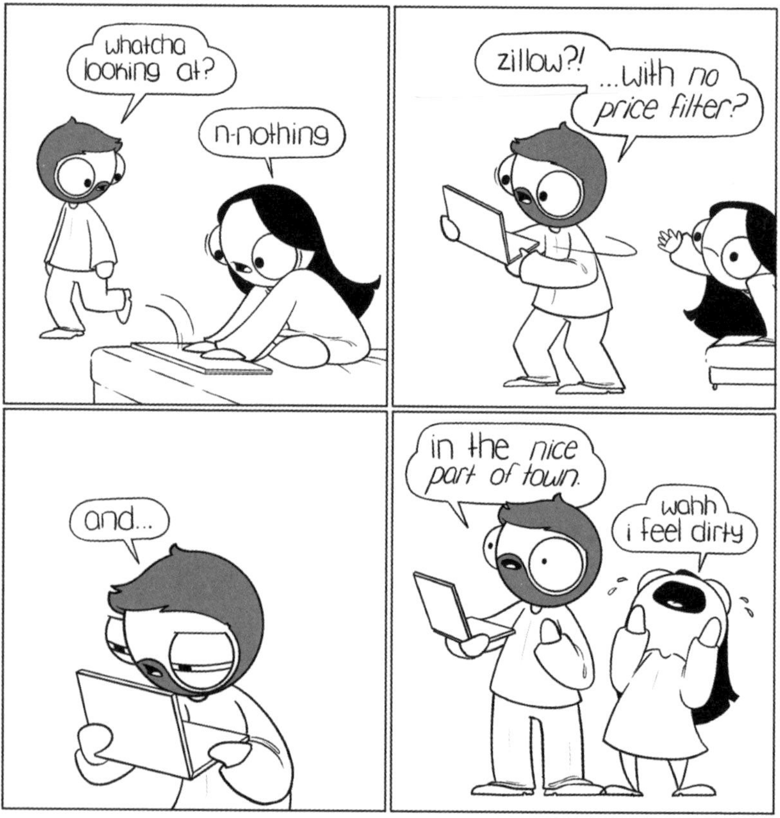
whatcha looking at?
n-nothing
zillow?!
...with *no price filter?*
and...
in the *nice part of town.*
wahh i feel dirty

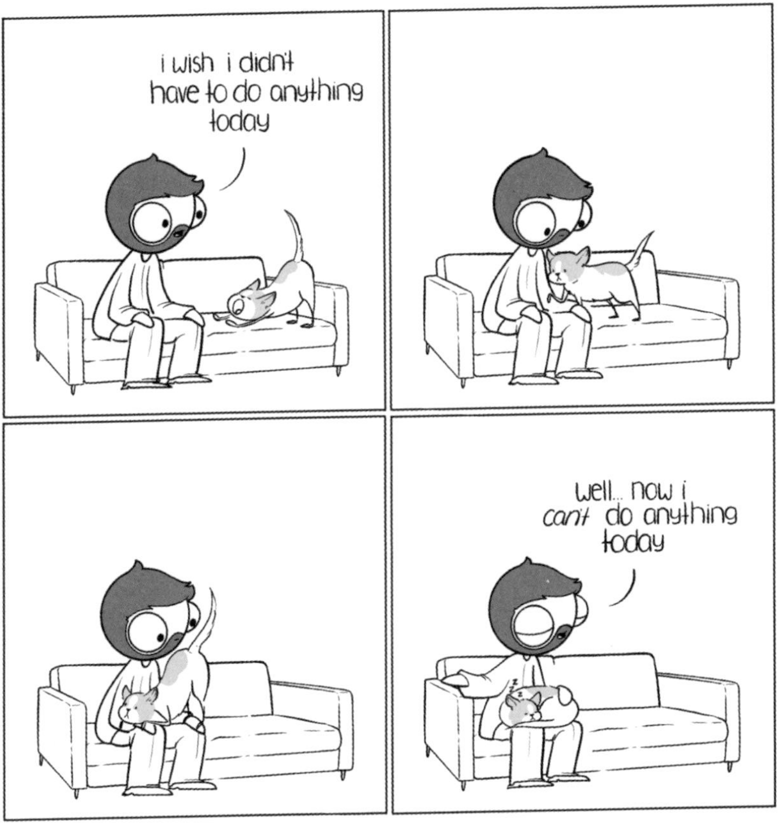
i wish i didn't have to do anything today
well... now i *can't* do anything today

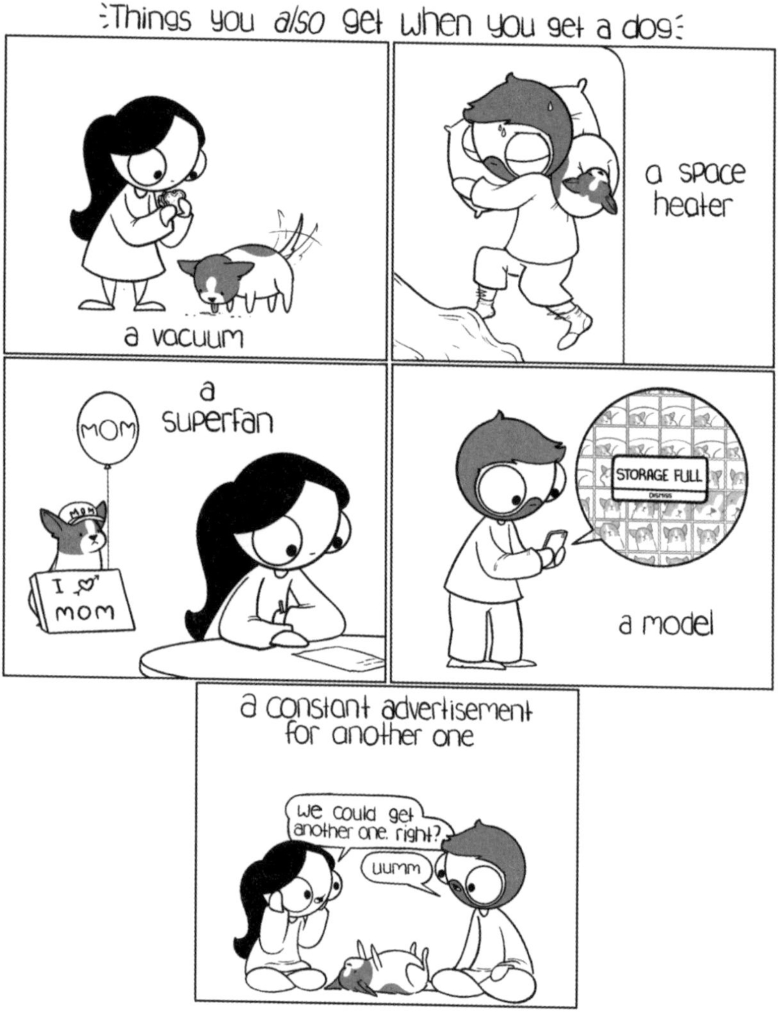
Things you *also* get when you get a dog
a vacuum
a space heater
MOM
a superfan
MOM
I ♥ MOM
STORAGE FULL
a model
a constant advertisement for another one
we could get another one. right?
uumm

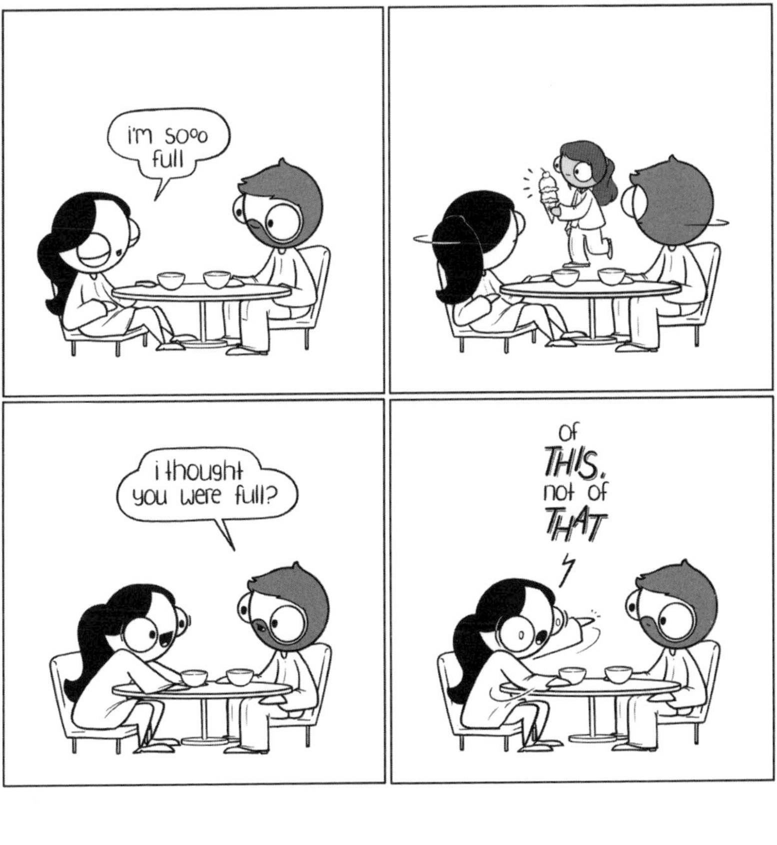
i'm sooo full
i thought you were full?
of THIS, not of THAT

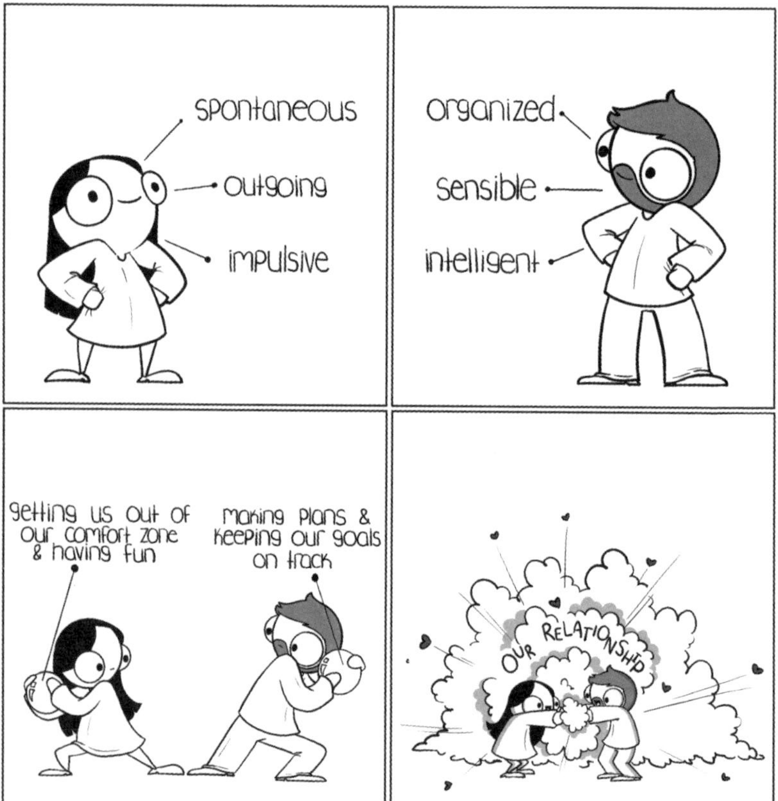
spontaneous
outgoing
impulsive
organized
sensible
intelligent
getting us out of our comfort zone & having fun
making plans & keeping our goals on track
OUR RELATIONSHIP

waiting mode

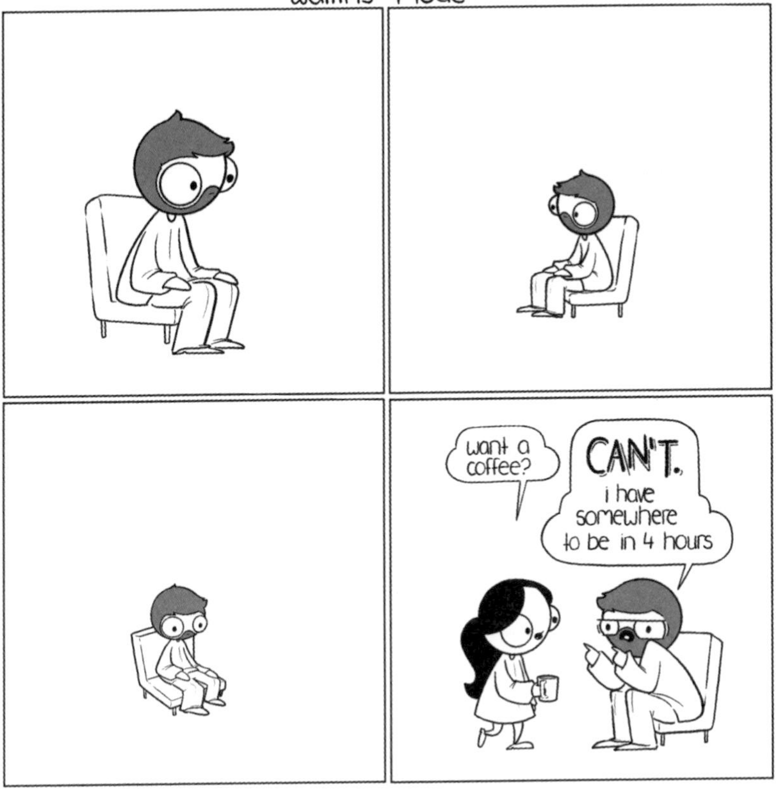
want a coffee?
CAN'T.
i have somewhere to be in 4 hours

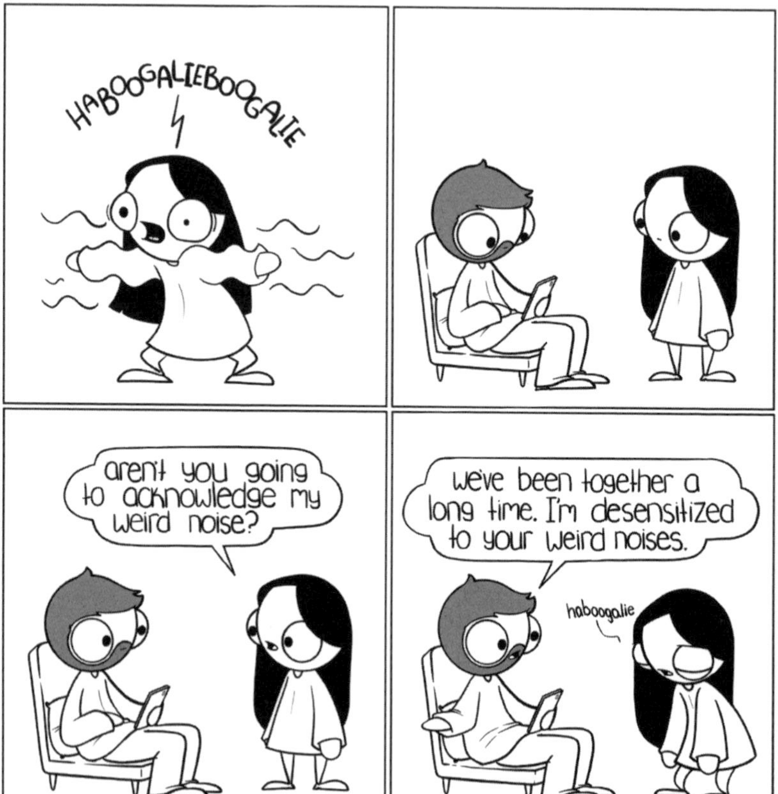
HABOOGALIEBOOGALIE
aren't you going to acknowledge my weird noise?
we've been together a long time. I'm desensitized to your weird noises.
haboogalie

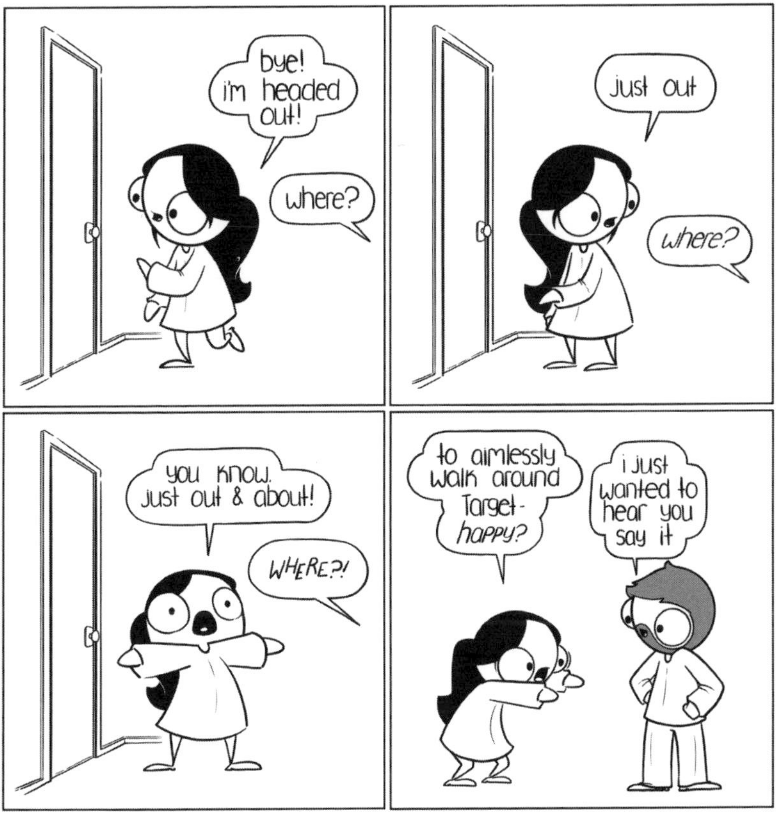
bye! i'm headed out!
where?
just out
where?
you know. just out & about!
WHERE?!
to aimlessly walk around Target- happy?
i just wanted to hear you say it

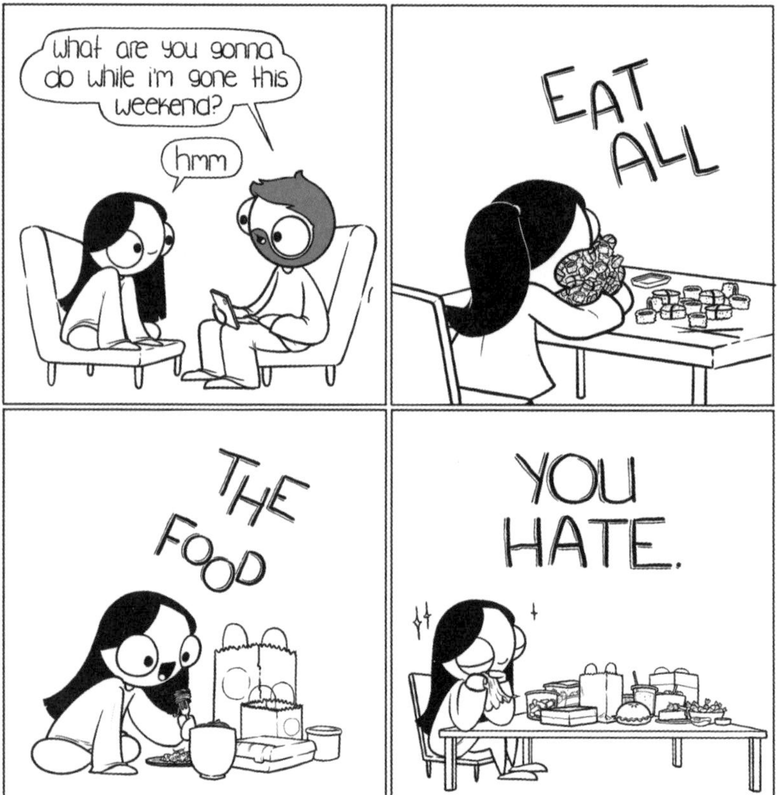
what are you gonna do while i'm gone this weekend?
hmm
EAT ALL
THE FOOD
YOU HATE.

the burrito cycle

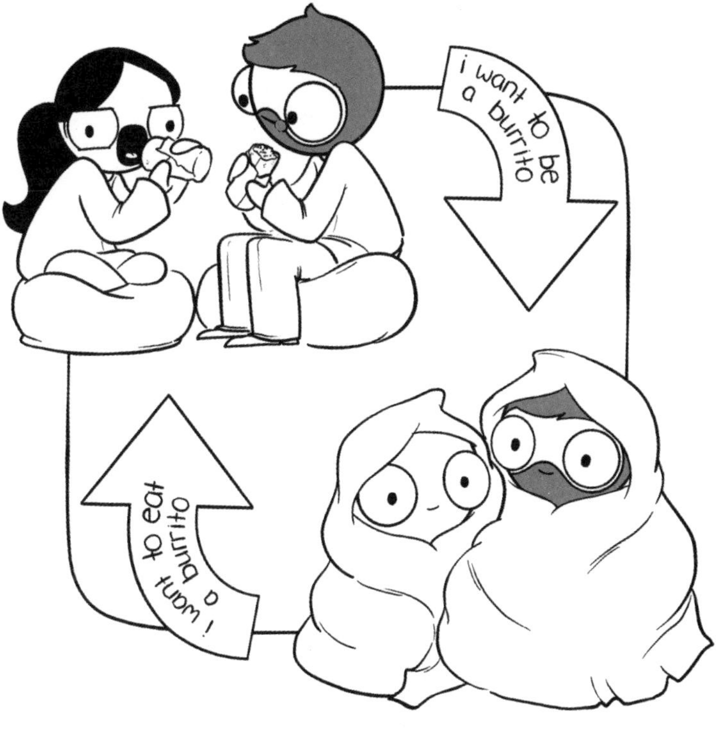

i want to be a burrito
i want to eat a burrito

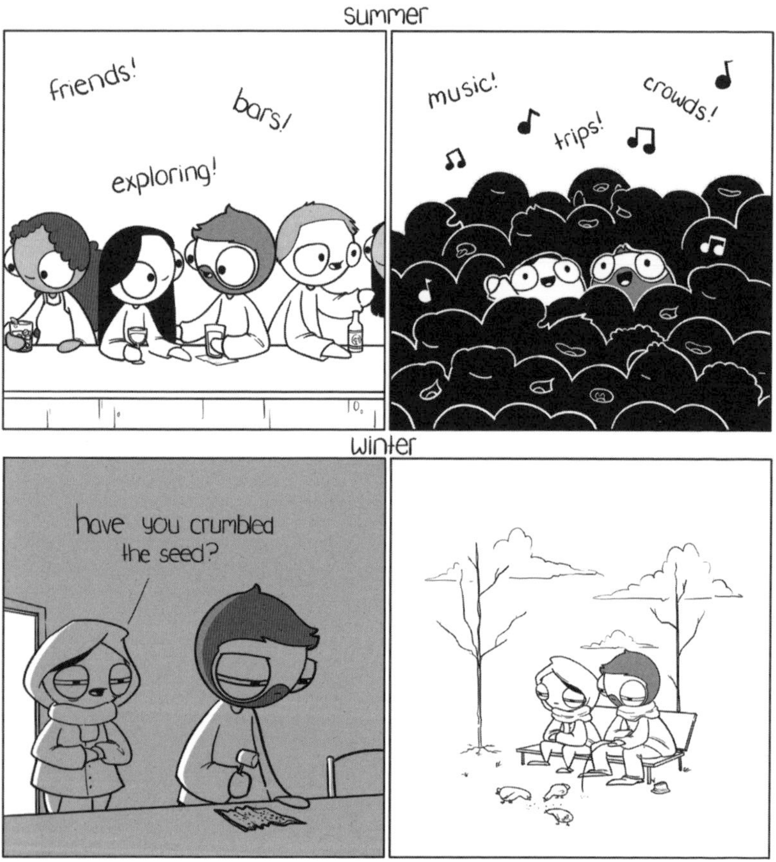
summer
friends!
bars!
exploring!
music!
trips!
crowds!
winter
have you crumbled the seed?

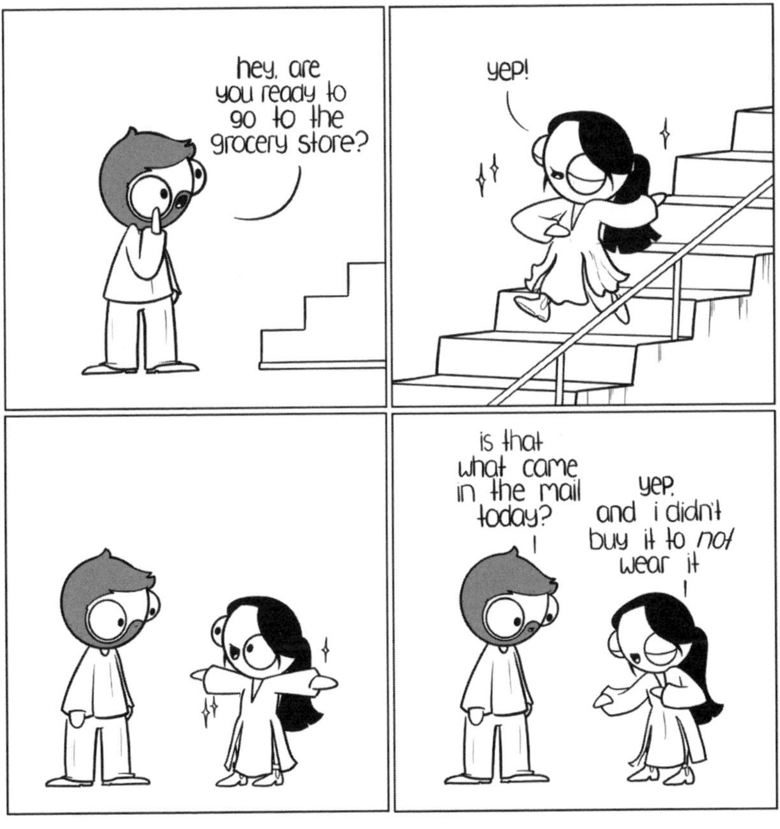
hey, are you ready to go to the grocery store?
yep!
is that what came in the mail today?
yep, and i didn't buy it to *not* wear it

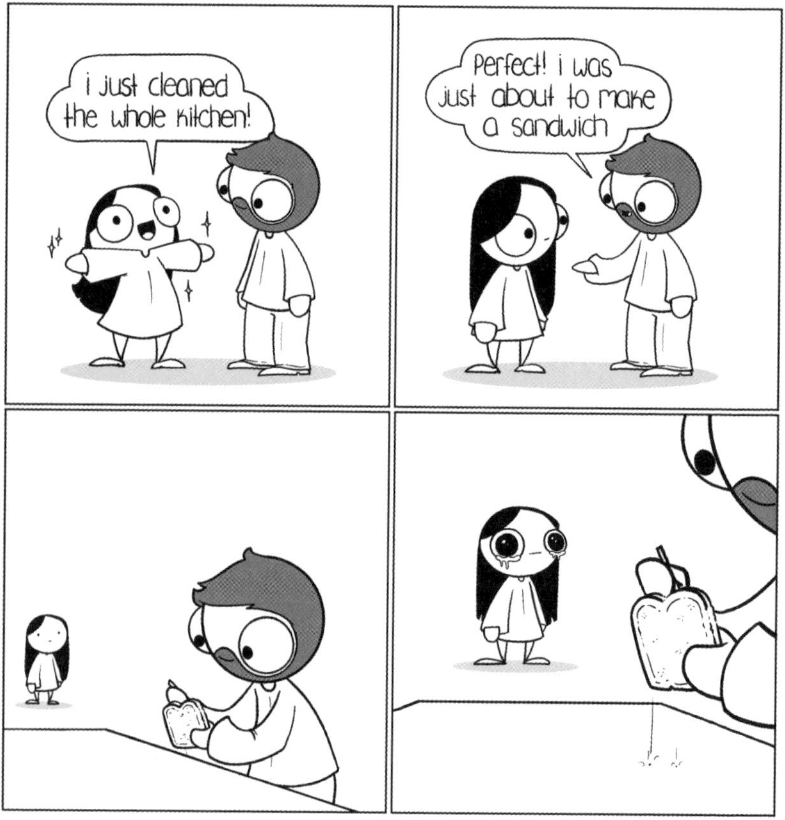
i just cleaned the whole kitchen!
Perfect! i was just about to make a sandwich

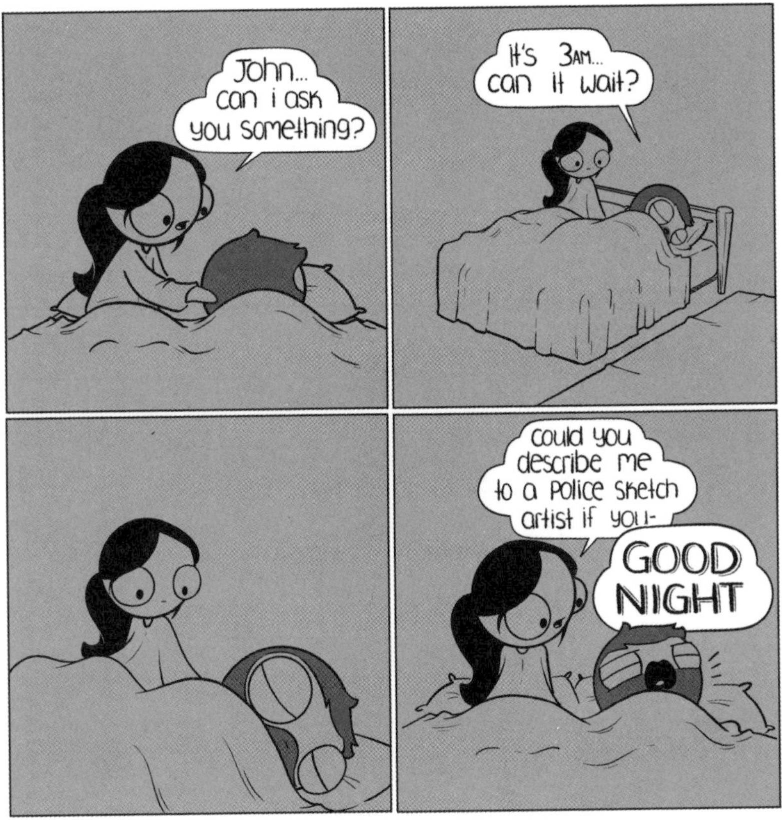
John...
can i ask
you something?
it's 3AM...
can it wait?
could you
describe me
to a police sketch
artist if you-
GOOD
NIGHT

"cheer up"

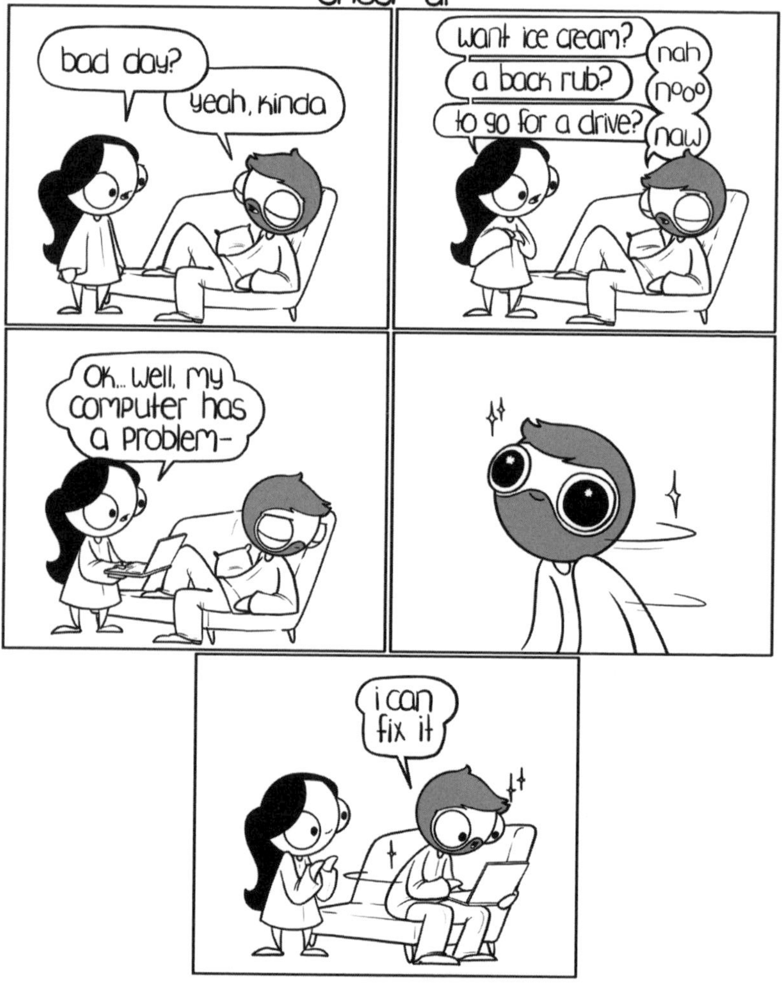
bad day?
yeah, kinda
want ice cream?
nah
a back rub?
nooo
to go for a drive?
naw
ok... well, my computer has a problem-
i can fix it

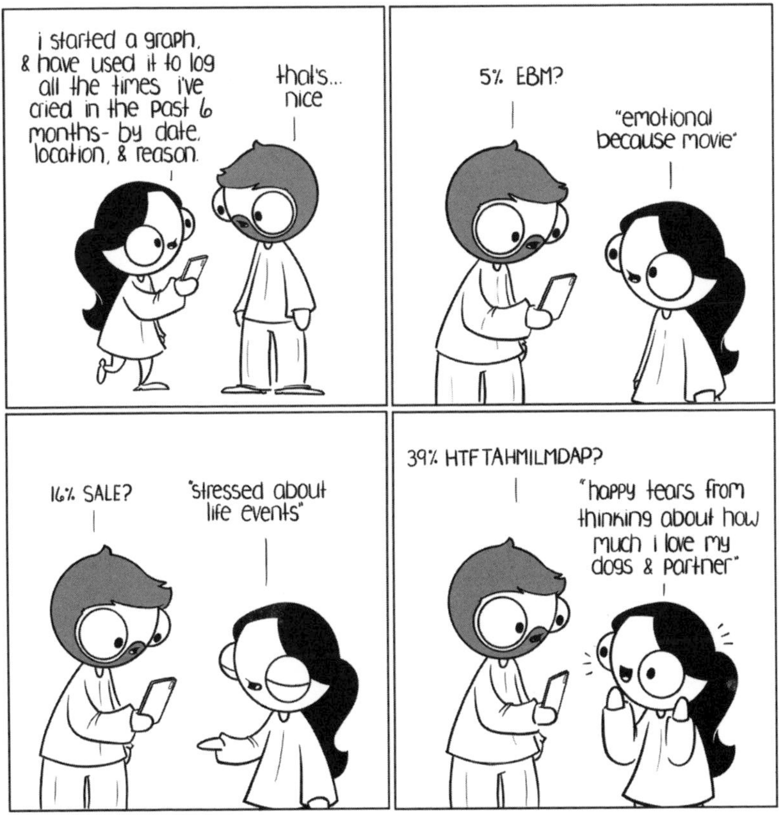
i started a graph, & have used it to log all the times i've cried in the past 6 months- by date, location, & reason.
that's... nice
5% EBM?
"emotional because movie"
16% SALE?
"stressed about life events"
39% HTFTAHMILMDAP?
"happy tears from thinking about how much i love my dogs & partner"

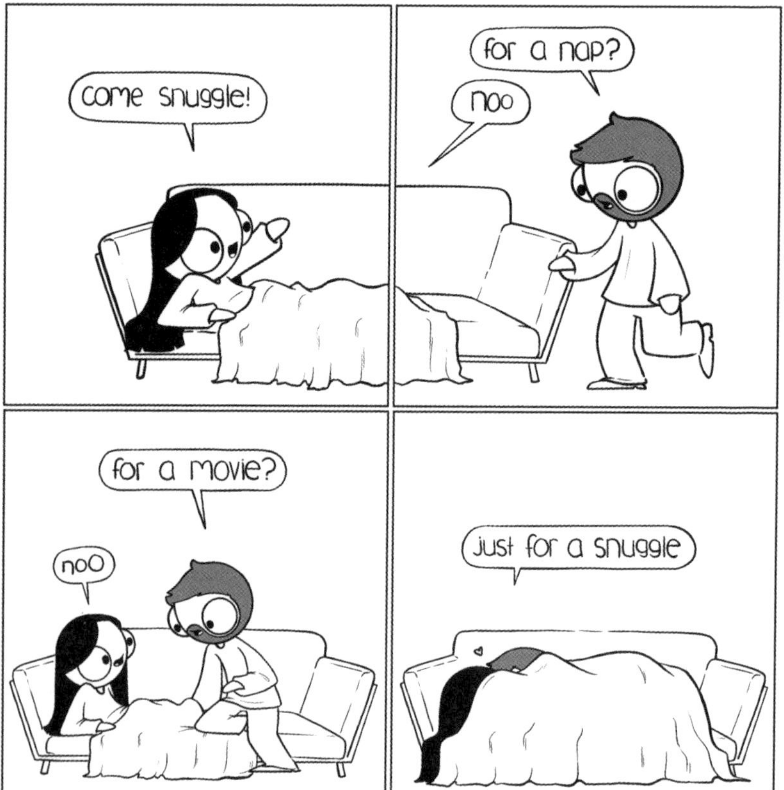
come snuggle!
for a nap?
noo
for a movie?
noO
just for a snuggle

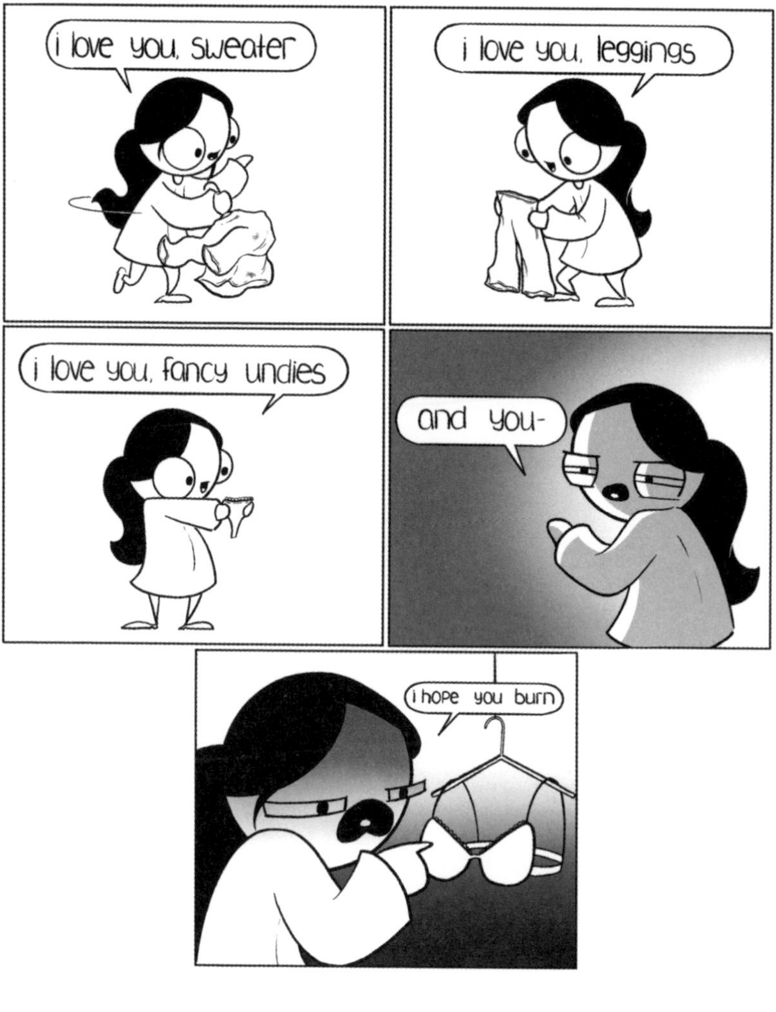
i love you, sweater
i love you, leggings
i love you, fancy undies
and you-
i hope you burn

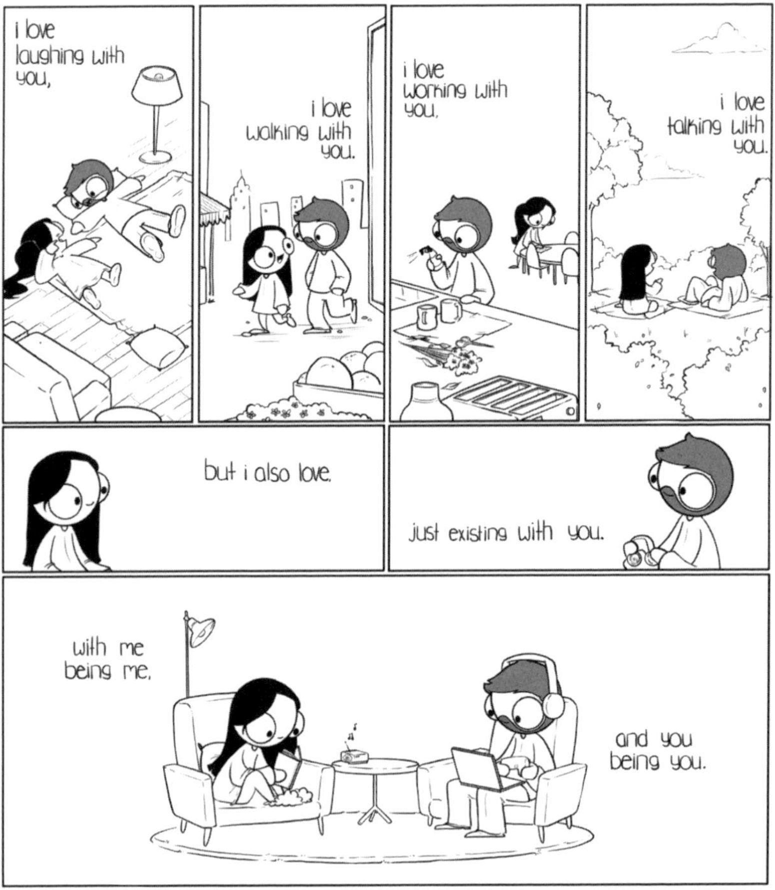
i love
laughing with
you,
i love
walking with
you.
i love
working with
you,
i love
talking with
you.
but i also love.
just existing with you.
with me
being me,
and you
being you.

when you want to be mysterious but you've been together forever

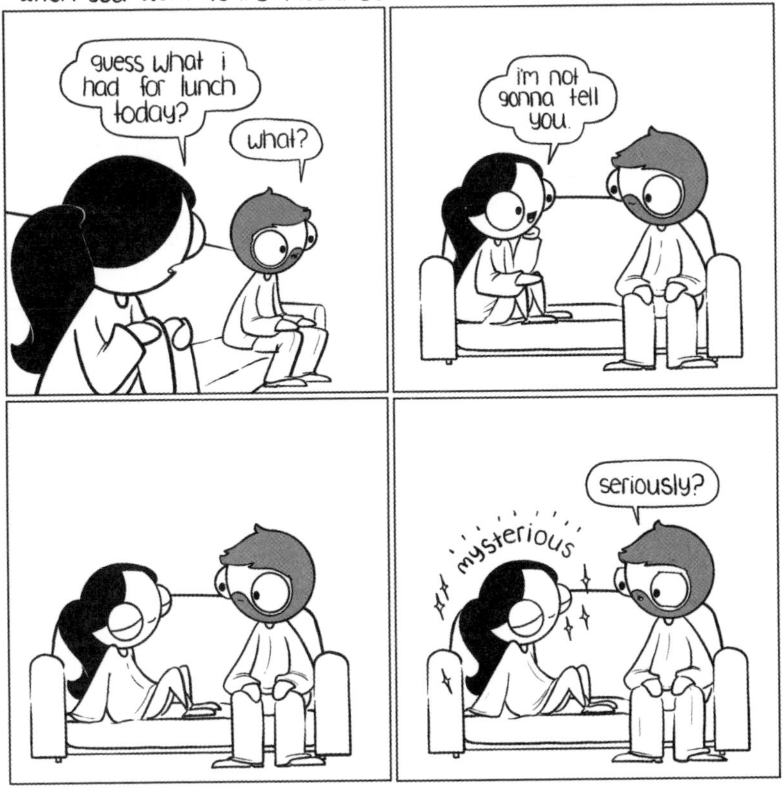
guess what i had for lunch today?
what?
i'm not gonna tell you.
mysterious
seriously?

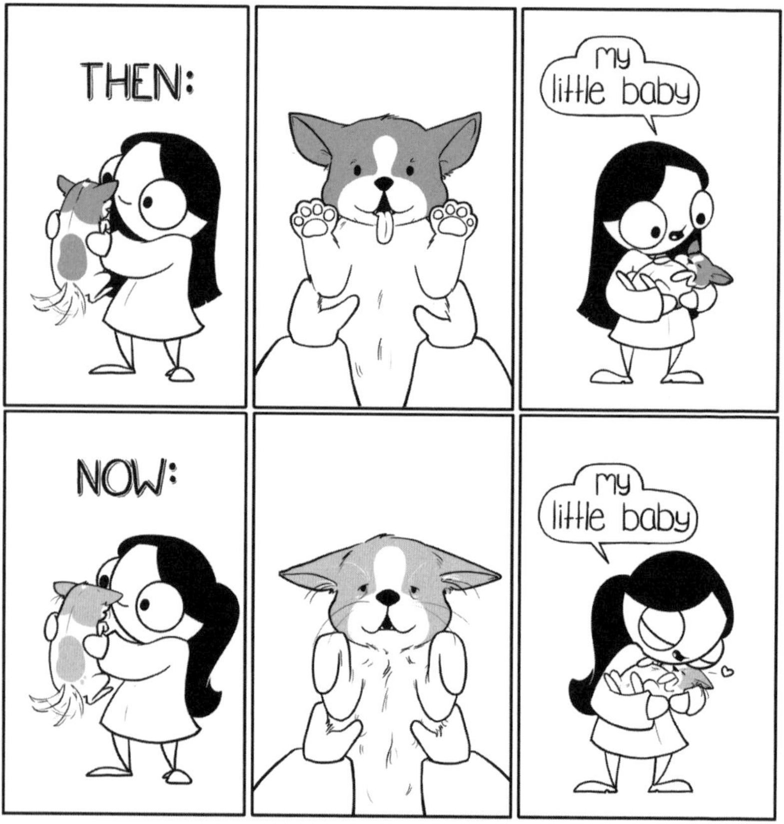
THEN:
my little baby
NOW:
my little baby

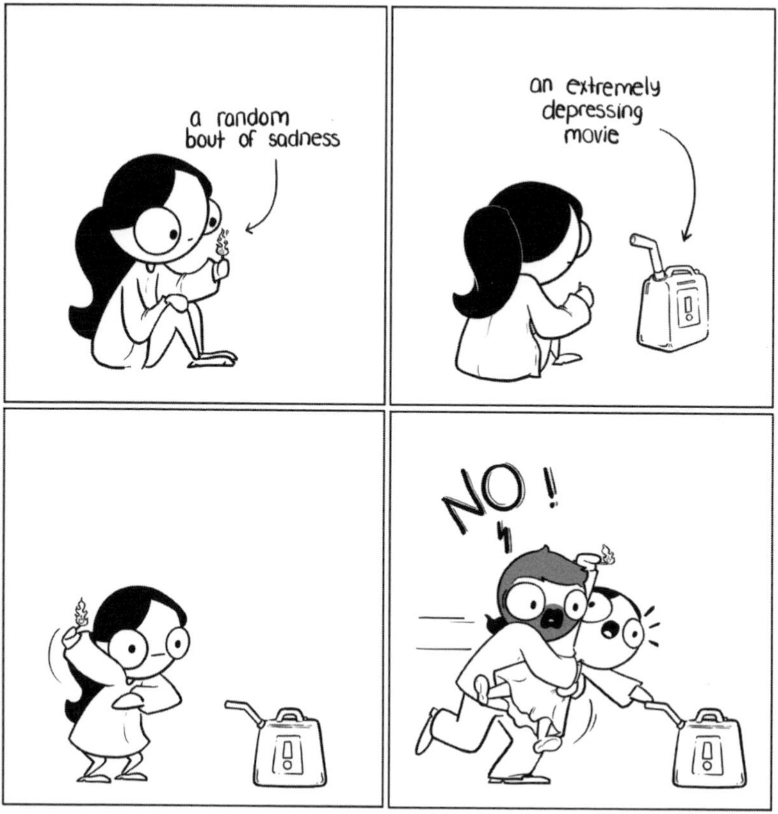
a random
bout of sadness
an extremely
depressing
movie
NO!!

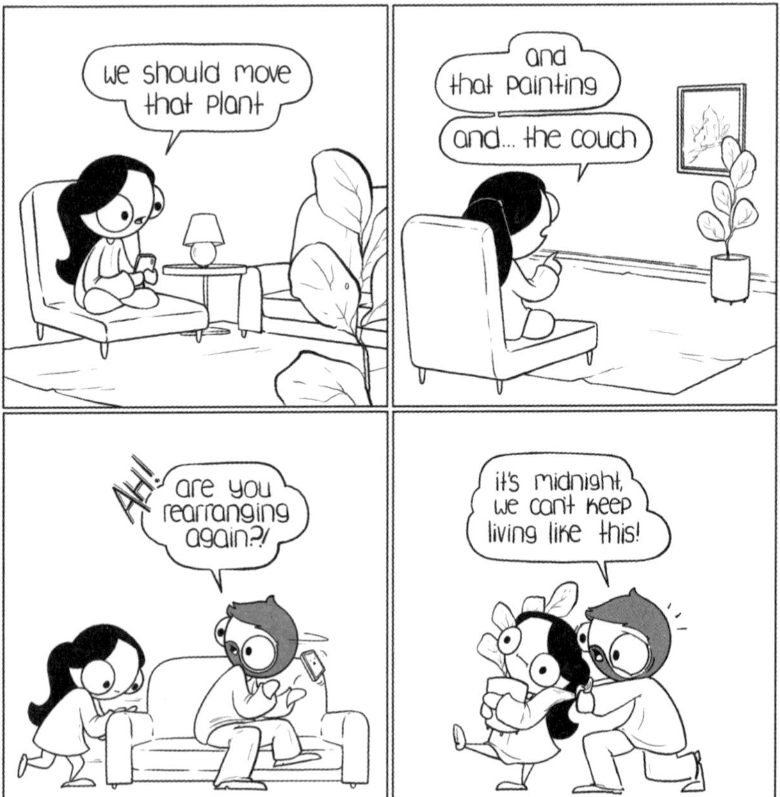
we should move that plant
and that painting
and... the couch
AH!
are you rearranging again?!
it's midnight, we can't keep living like this!

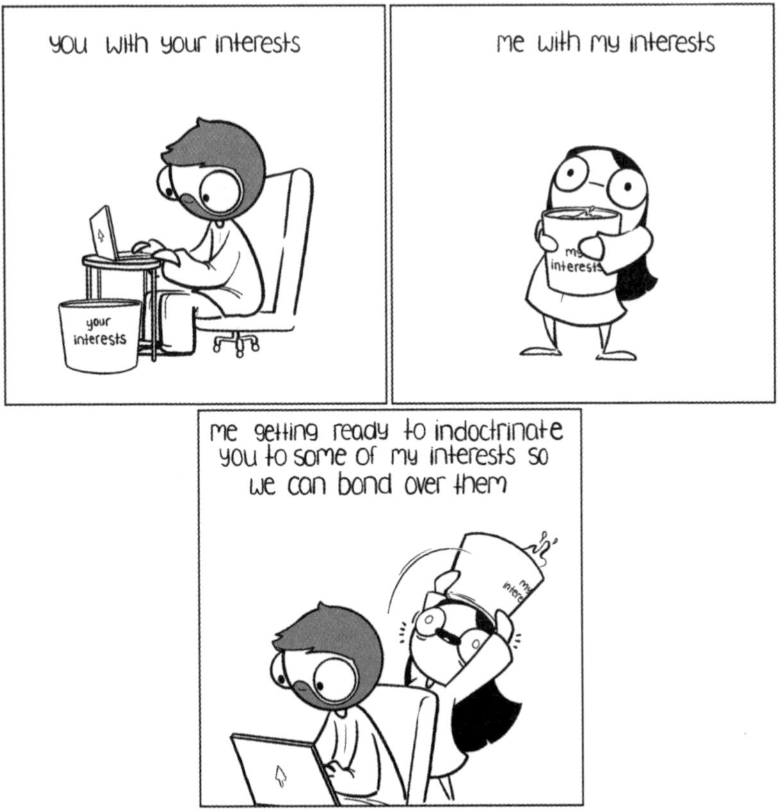
you with your interests
your interests
me with my interests
my interests
me getting ready to indoctrinate you to some of my interests so we can bond over them

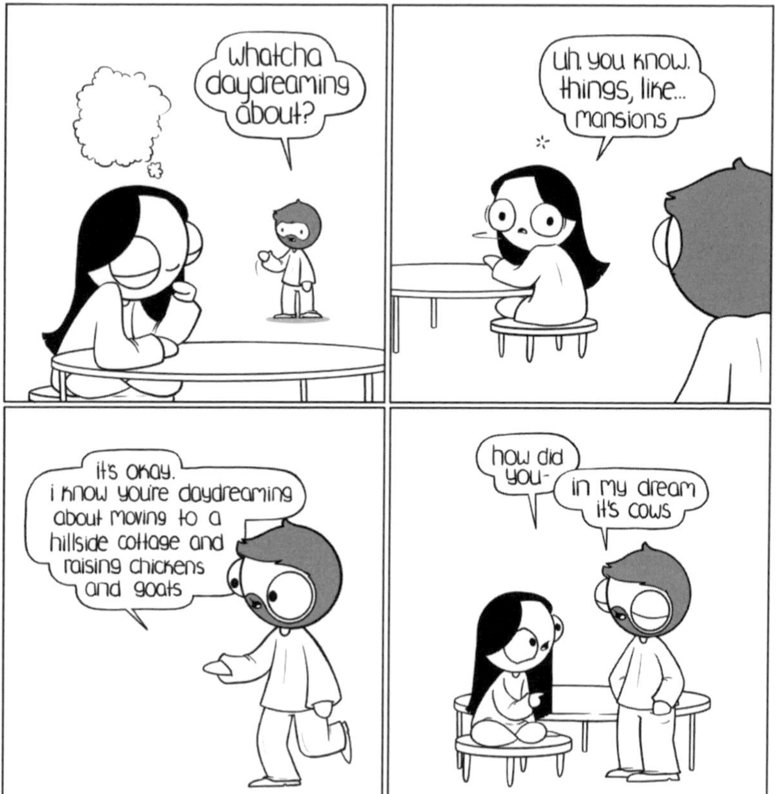
whatcha daydreaming about?
uh. you know. things, like... mansions
it's okay. i know you're daydreaming about moving to a hillside cottage and raising chickens and goats
how did you-
in my dream it's cows

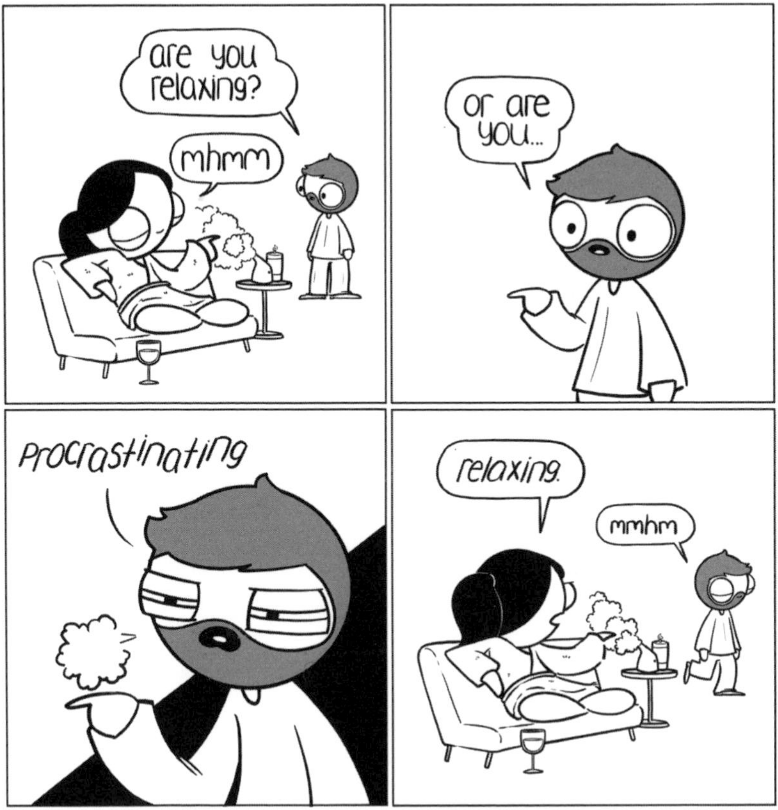
are you relaxing?
mhmm
or are you...
Procrastinating
relaxing.
mmhm

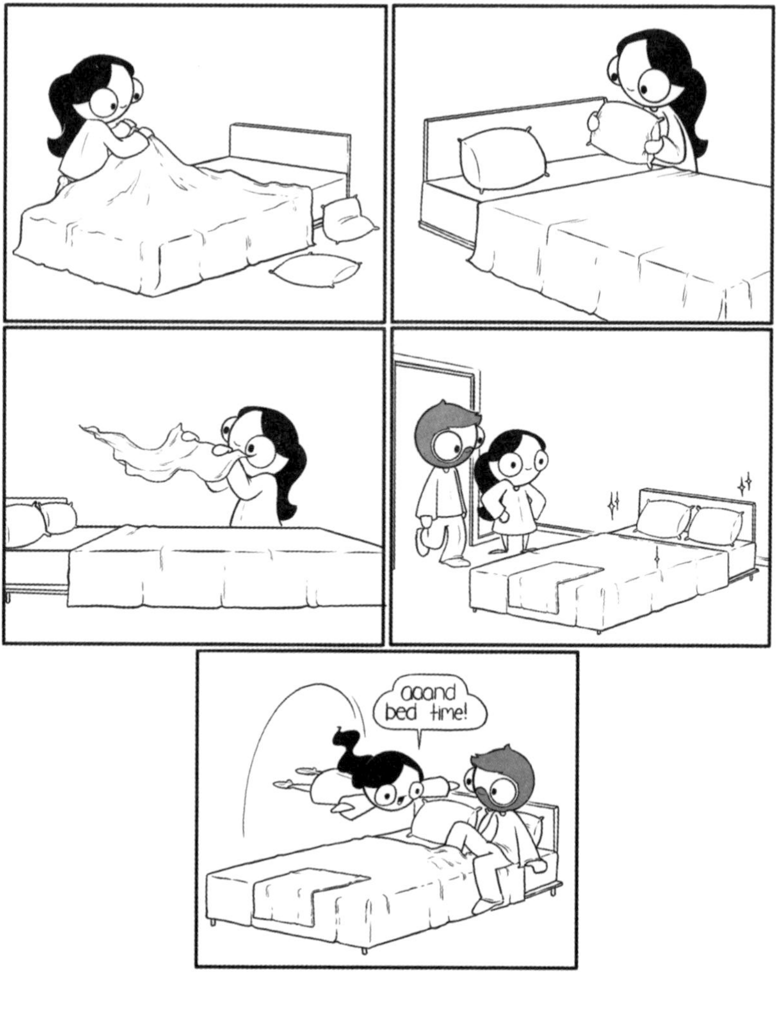
aaand bed time!

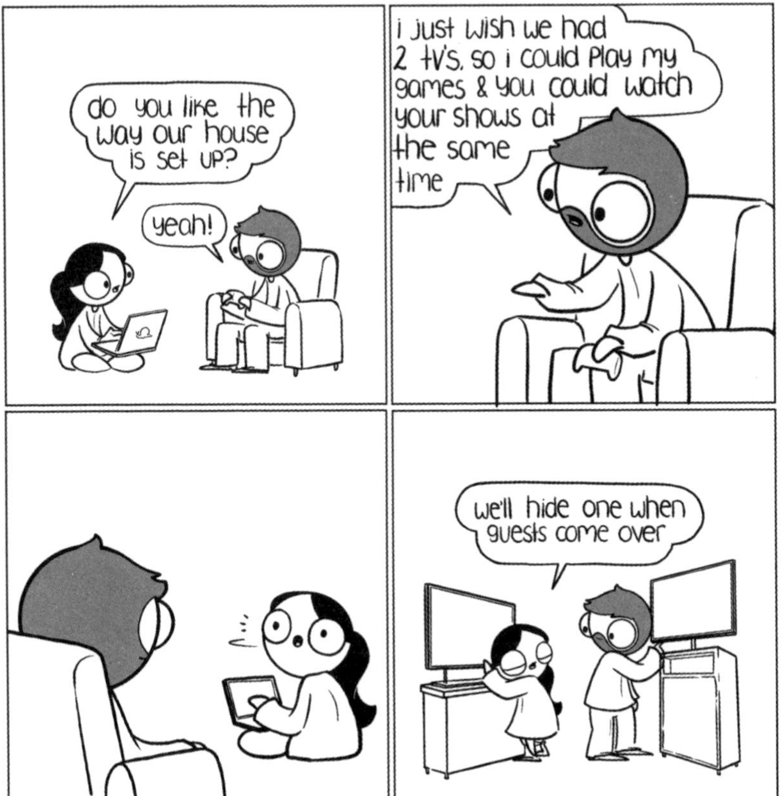
do you like the way our house is set up?
yeah!
i just wish we had 2 tv's, so i could play my games & you could watch your shows at the same time
we'll hide one when guests come over

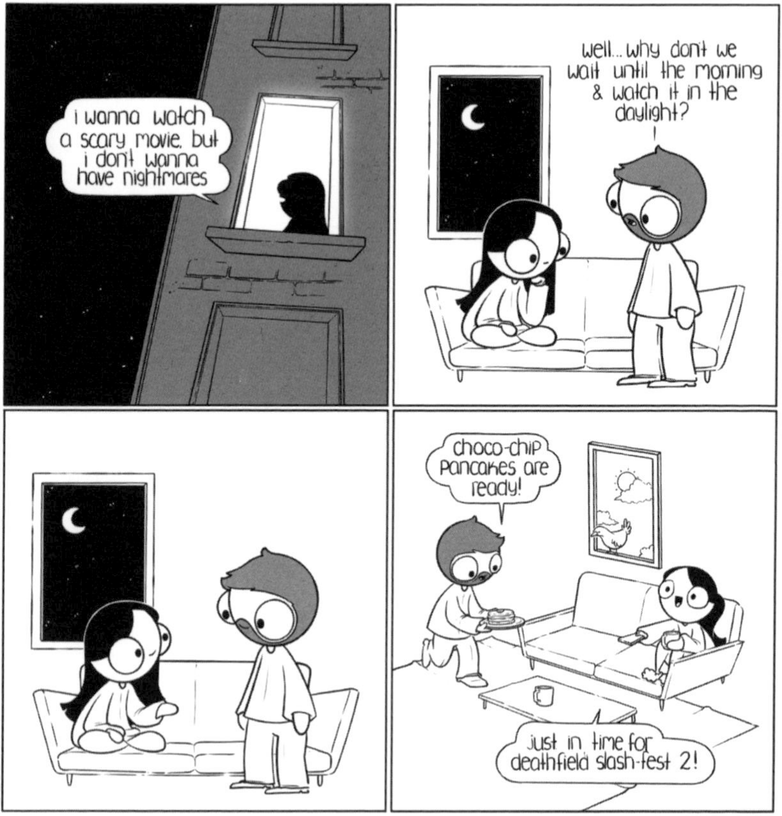
i wanna watch a scary movie. but i don't wanna have nightmares
well... why don't we wait until the morning & watch it in the daylight?
choco-chip pancakes are ready!
just in time for deathfield slash-fest 2!

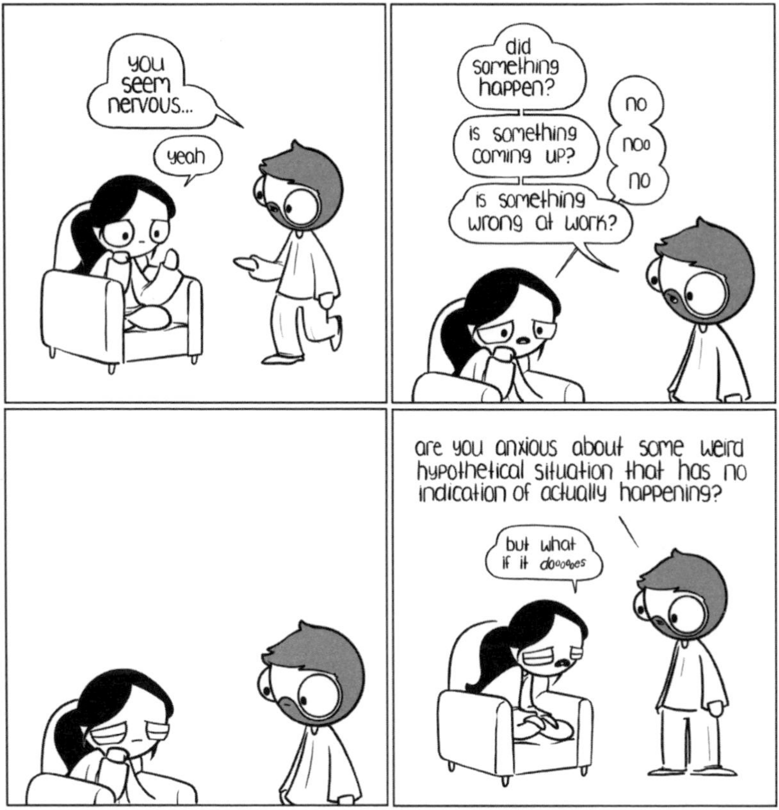
you seem nervous...
yeah
did something happen?
no
is something coming up?
noo
is something wrong at work?
no
are you anxious about some weird hypothetical situation that has no indication of actually happening?
but what if it doooooes

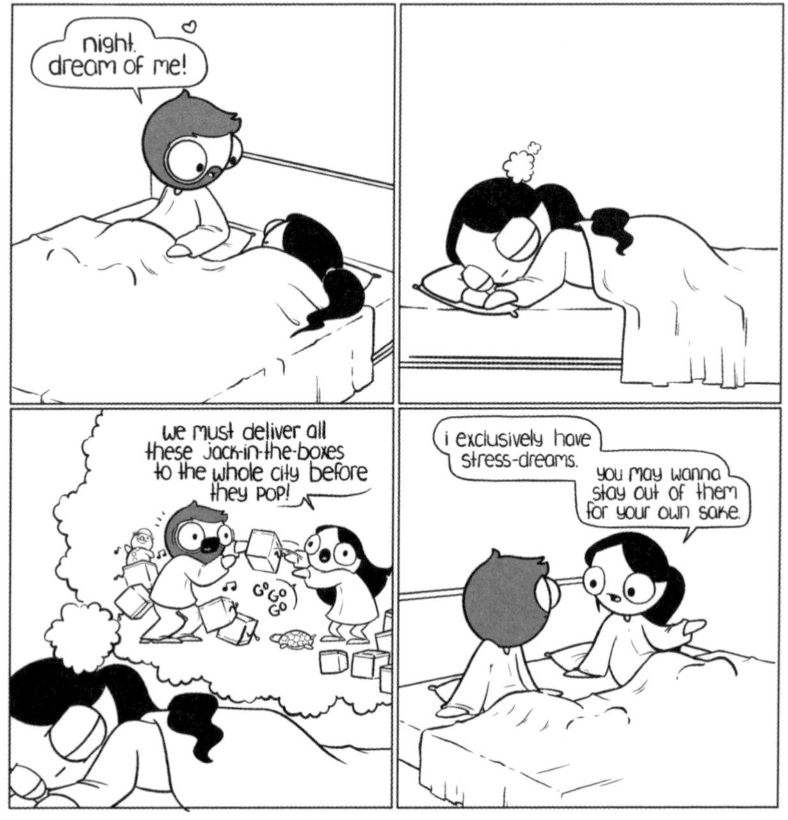
night.
dream of me!
we must deliver all these jack-in-the-boxes to the whole city before they pop!
GO GO GO
i exclusively have stress-dreams.
you may wanna stay out of them for your own sake.

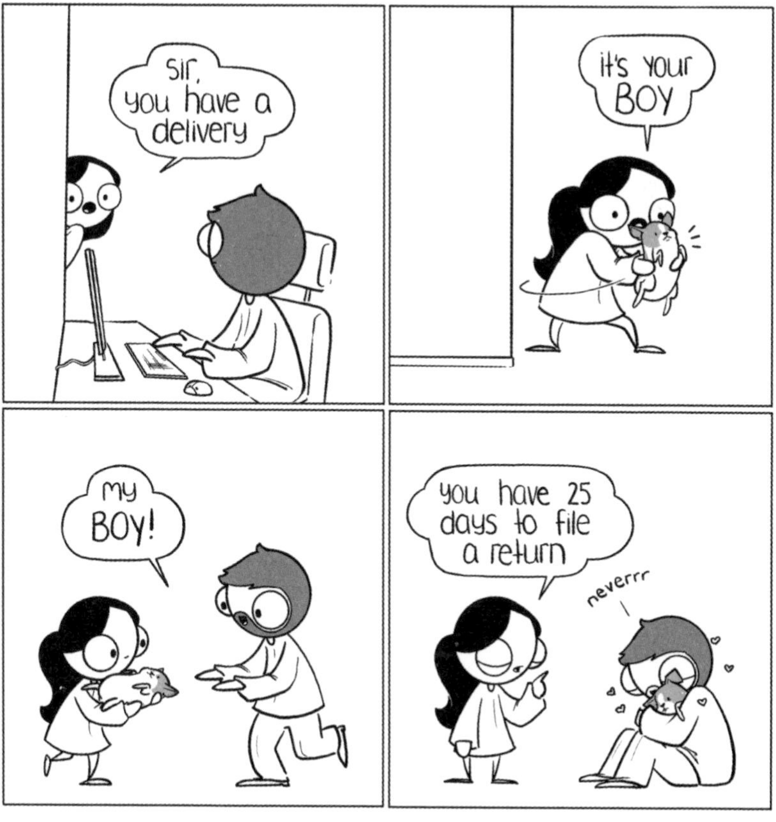
sir, you have a delivery
it's your BOY
my BOY!
you have 25 days to file a return
neverrr

can i ask you for some advice?
more specifically, can i ask you to reaffirm a decision ive already made so i don't feel like the sole person responsible for the outcome of my choices
I-

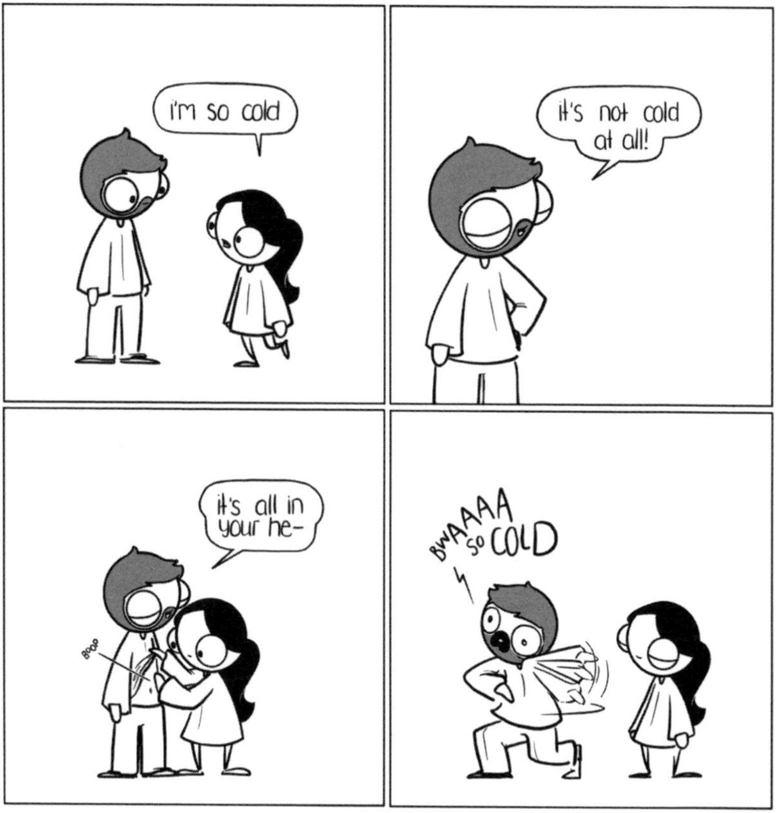
i'm so cold
it's not cold at all!
it's all in your he-
BOOP
BWAAAA so COLD

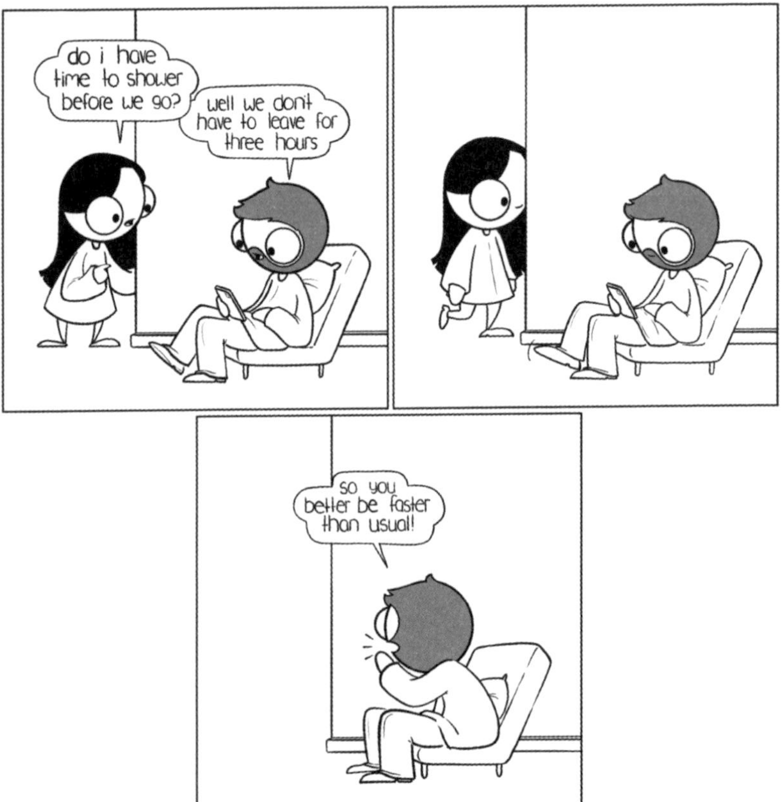
do i have time to shower before we go?
well we don't have to leave for three hours
so you better be faster than usual!

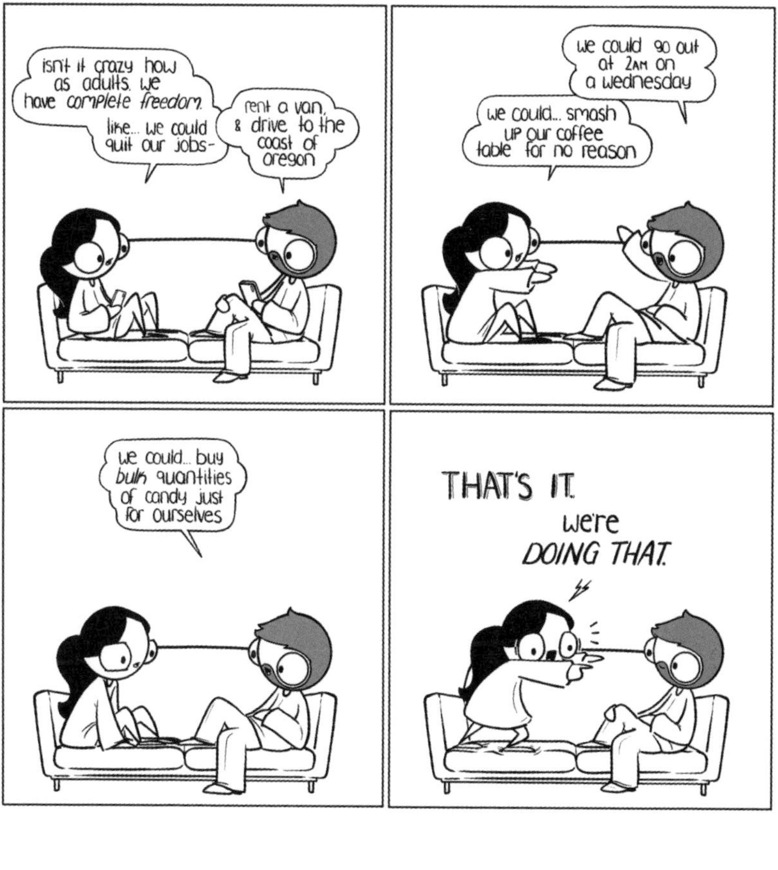
isn't it crazy how as adults, we have *complete freedom.*
like... we could quit our jobs-
rent a van, & drive to the coast of oregon
we could go out at 2AM on a wednesday
we could... smash up our coffee table for no reason
we could... buy *bulk* quantities of candy just for ourselves
THAT'S IT.
we're *DOING THAT.*

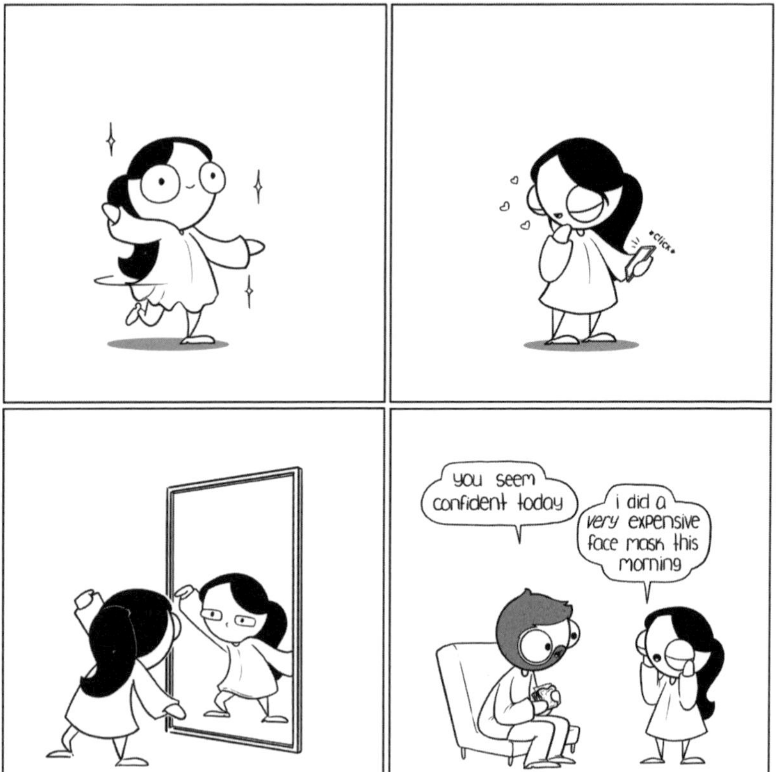
click
you seem confident today
i did a *very* expensive face mask this morning

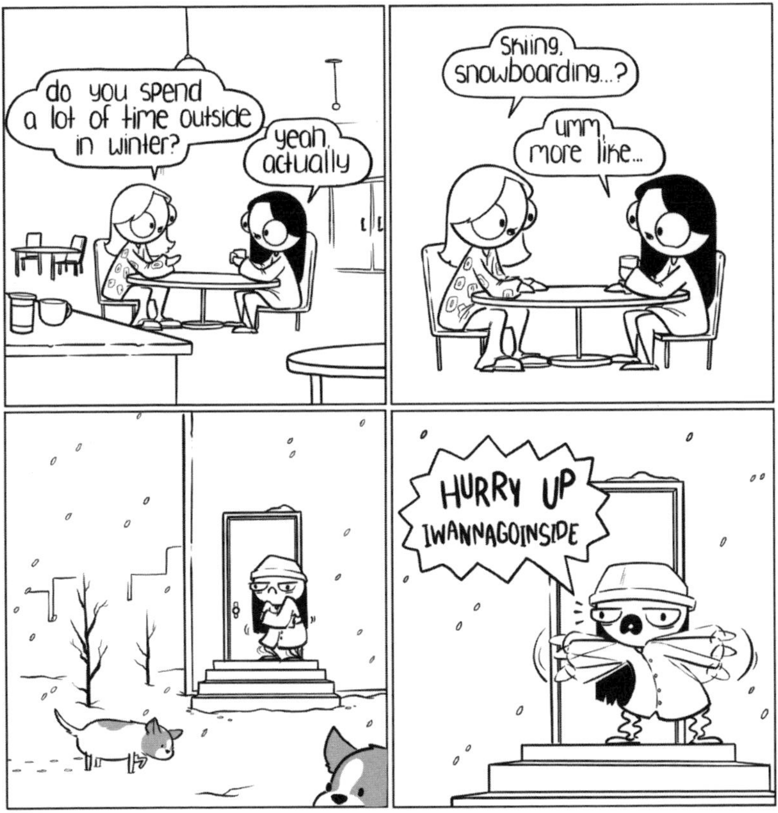
do you spend a lot of time outside in winter?
yeah, actually
Skiing, snowboarding...?
umm, more like...
HURRY UP
IWANNAGOINSIDE

music taste

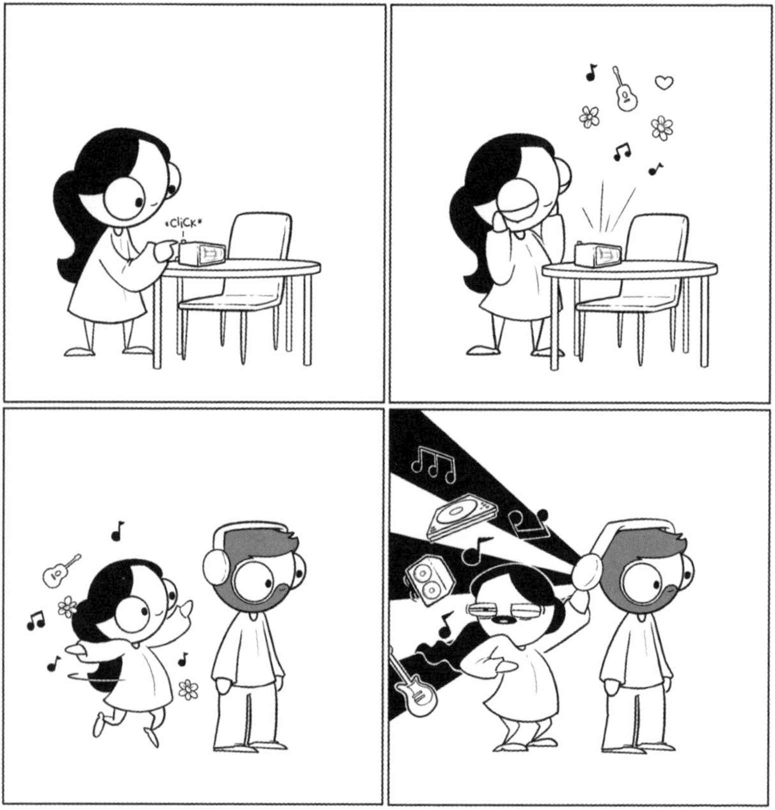
CLICK

Reasons why i can't sleep

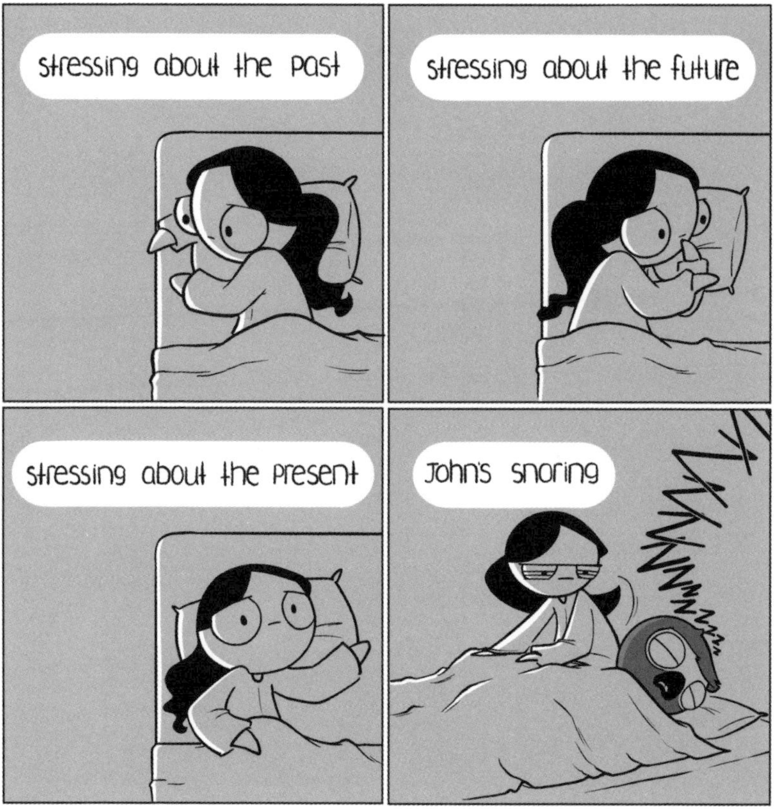
stressing about the past
stressing about the future
stressing about the present
John's snoring

signs your person is a pumpkin:

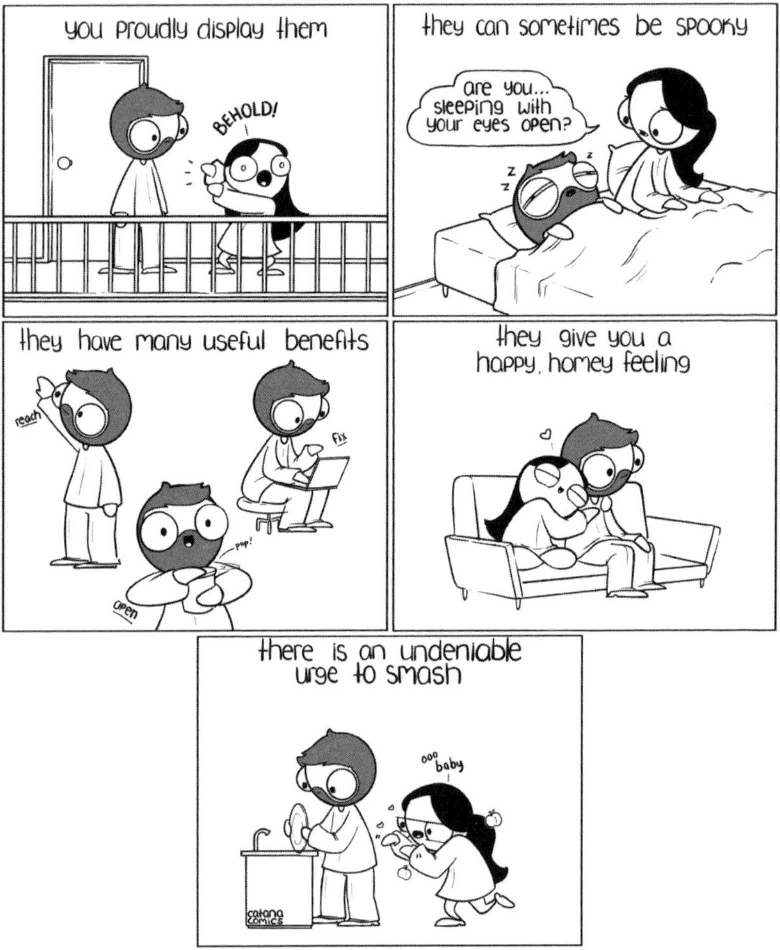

you proudly display them
BEHOLD!
they can sometimes be spooky
are you... sleeping with your eyes open?
z z z
they have many useful benefits
reach
fix
pop!
open
they give you a happy, homey feeling
there is an undeniable urge to smash
ooo baby
catana comics

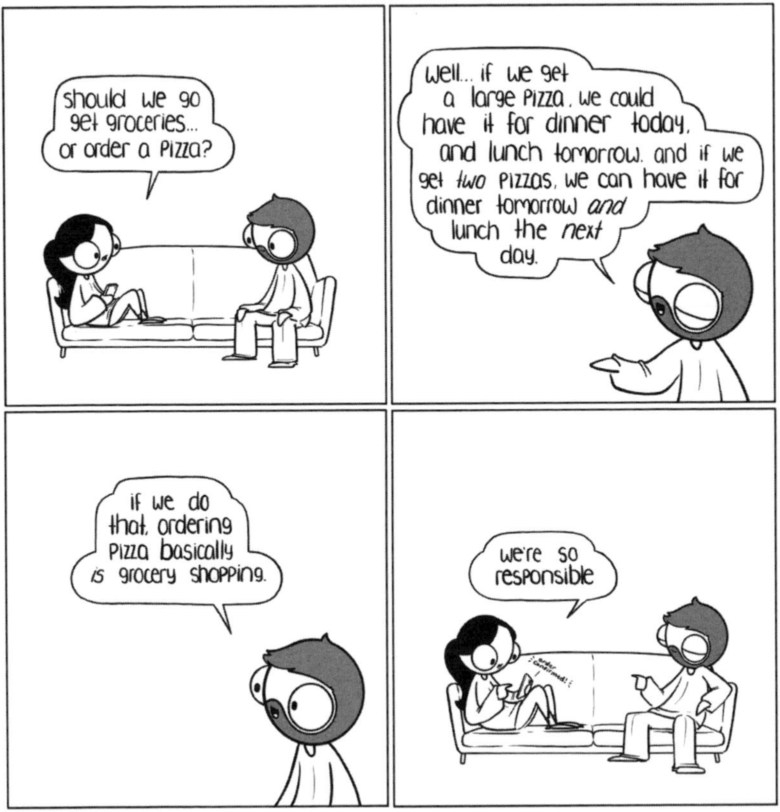
should we go get groceries... or order a pizza?
well... if we get a large pizza, we could have it for dinner today, and lunch tomorrow. and if we get *two* pizzas, we can have it for dinner tomorrow *and* lunch the *next* day.
if we do that, ordering pizza basically *is* grocery shopping.
order confirmed!
we're so responsible

reasons why i love wearing your clothes

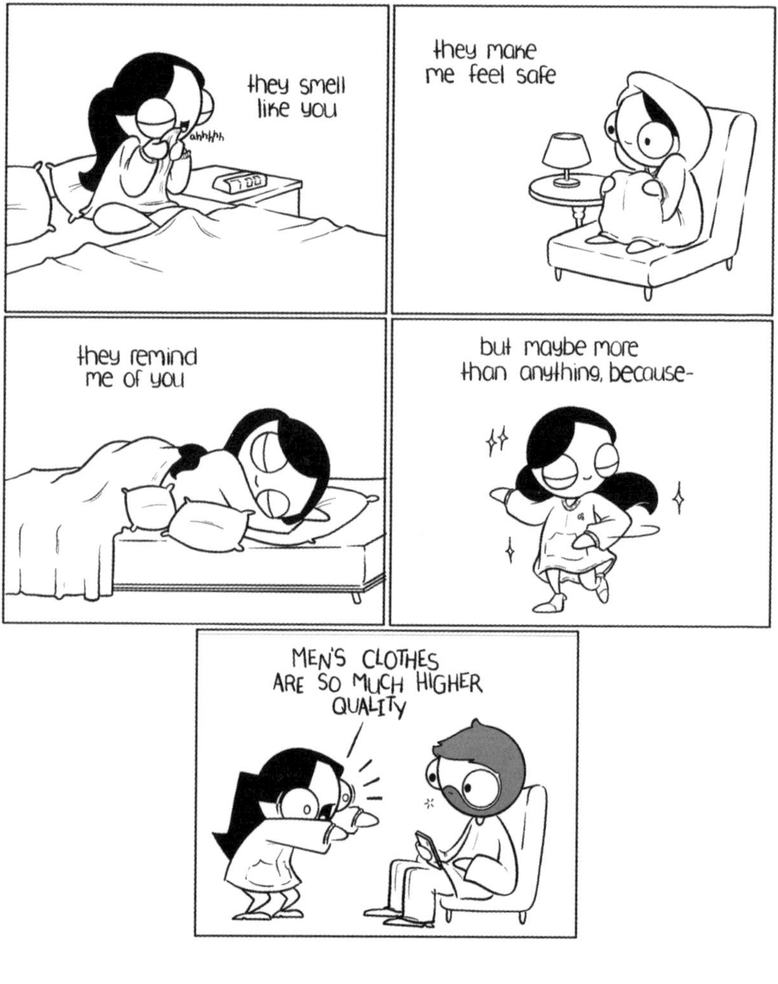
they smell like you
ahhhhh
they make me feel safe
they remind me of you
but maybe more than anything, because-
MEN'S CLOTHES ARE SO MUCH HIGHER QUALITY

clothes shopping

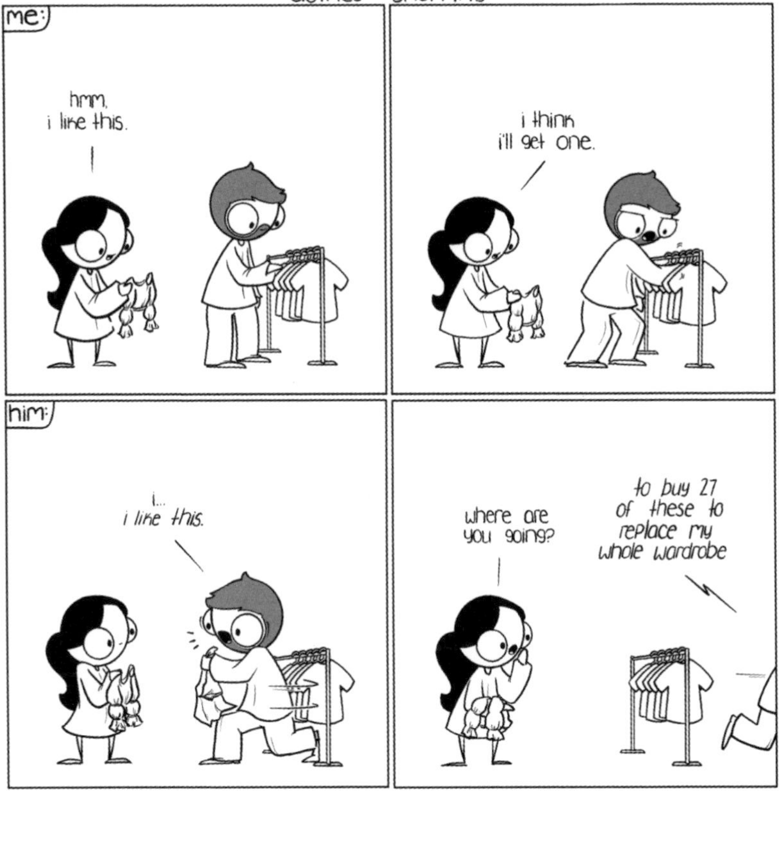
me:
hmm,
i like this.
i think
i'll get one.
him:
i...
i like this.
where are
you going?
to buy 27
of these to
replace my
whole wardrobe

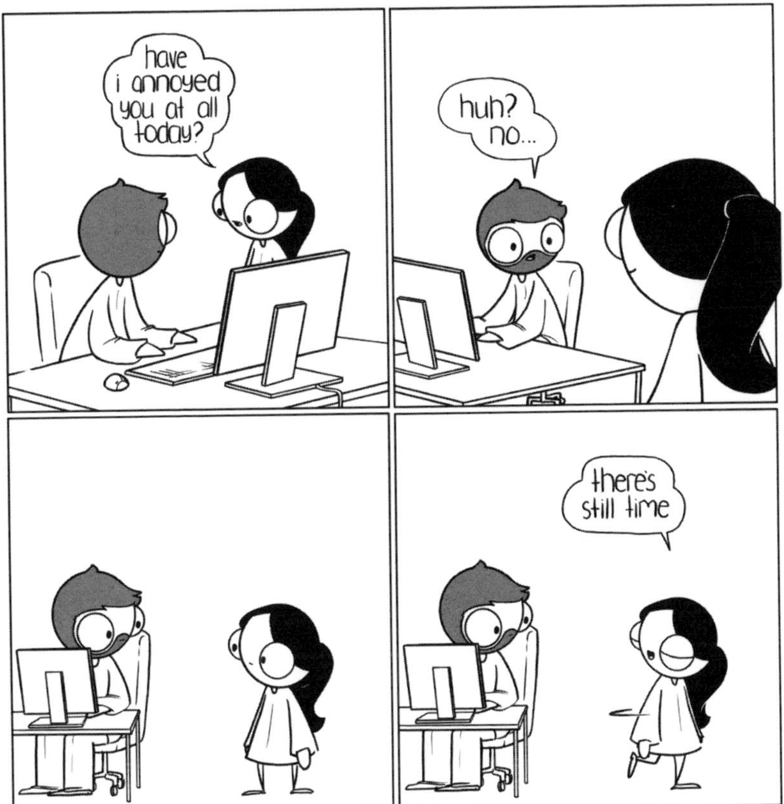
have i annoyed you at all today?
huh? no...
there's still time

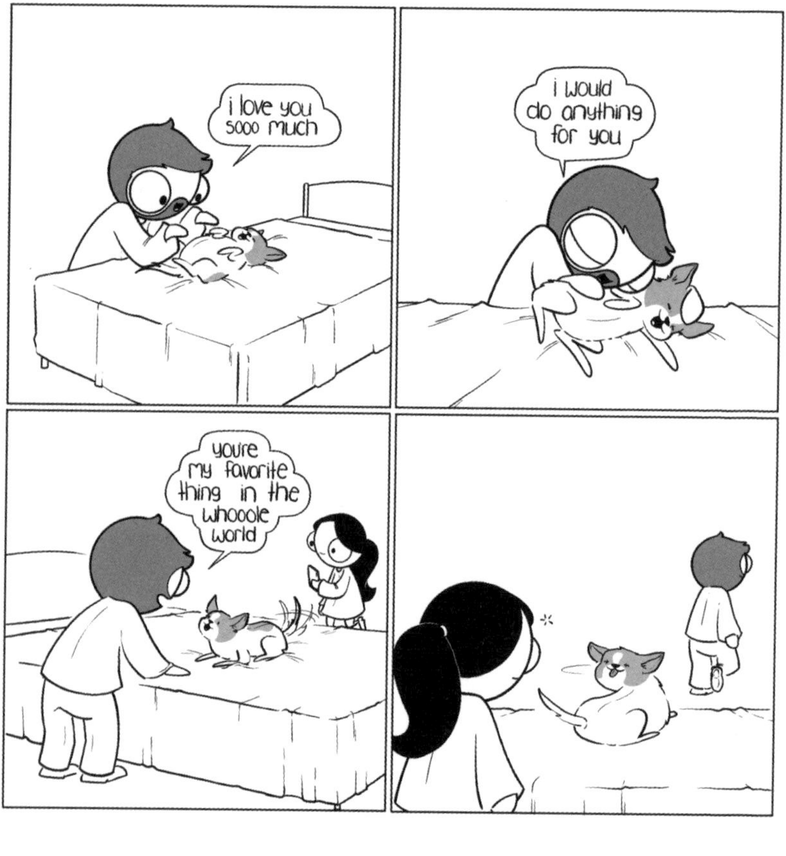
i love you sooo much
i would do anything for you
you're my favorite thing in the whooole world

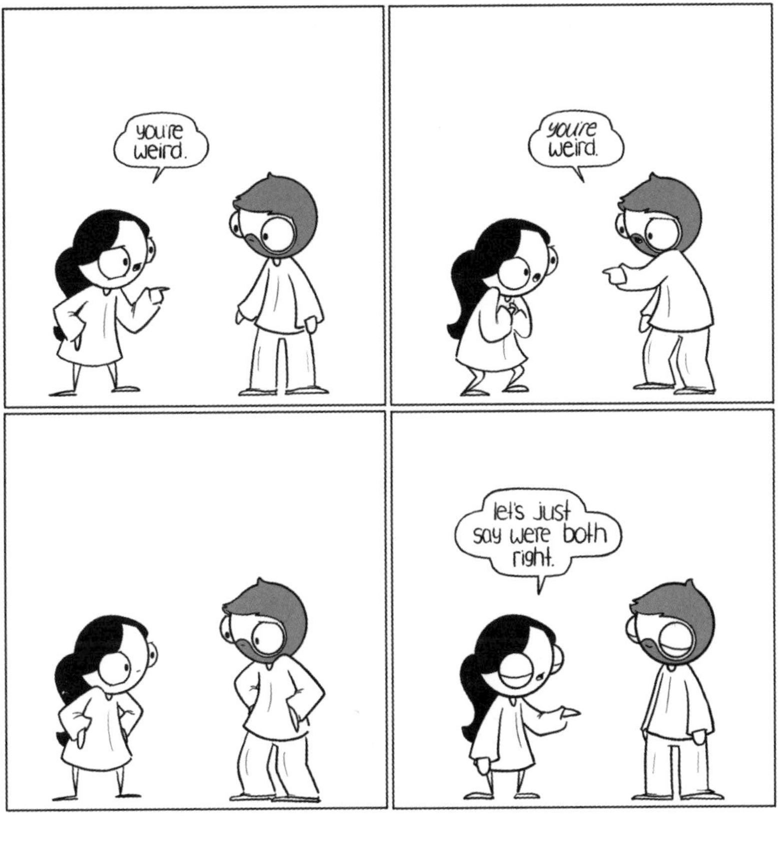
you're weird.
you're weird.
let's just say were both right.

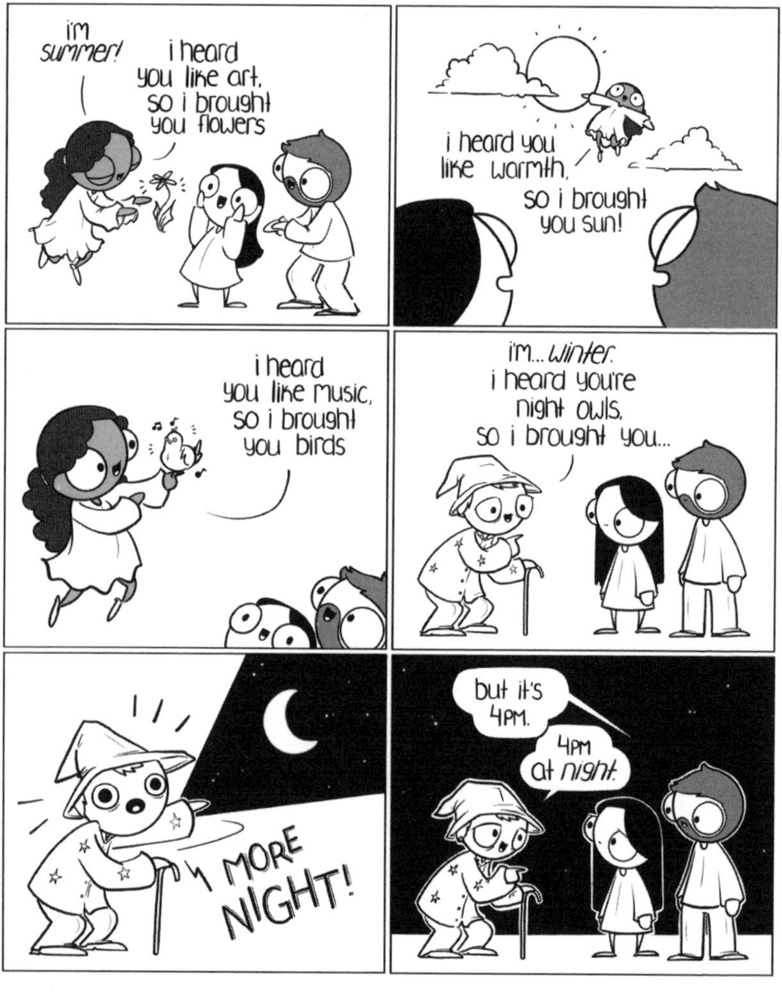
i'm summer!
i heard you like art, so i brought you flowers
i heard you like warmth, so i brought you sun!
i heard you like music, so i brought you birds
i'm... winter. i heard you're night owls, so i brought you...
MORE NIGHT!
but it's 4PM.
4PM at night.

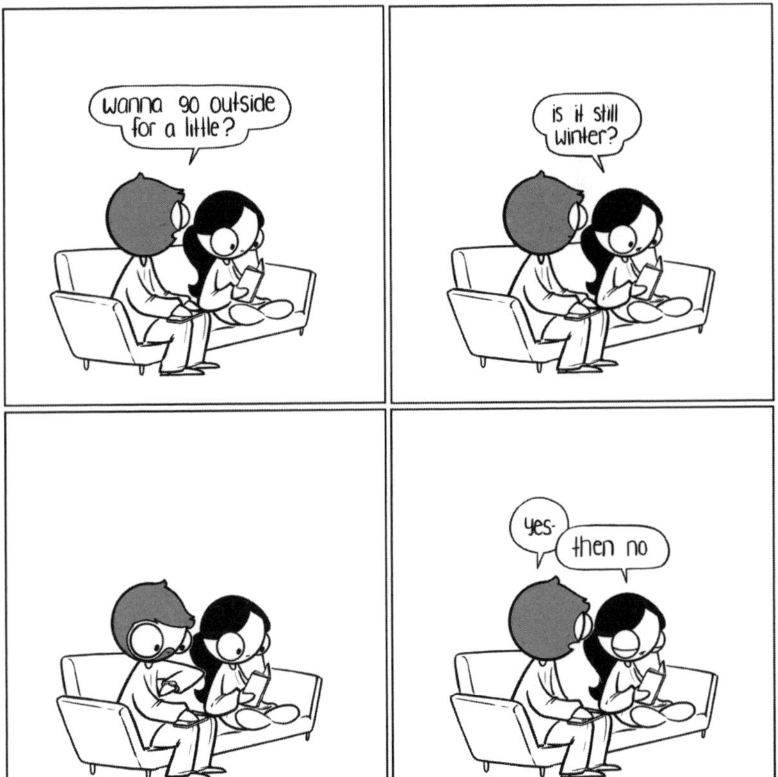
wanna go outside for a little?
is it still winter?
yes-
then no

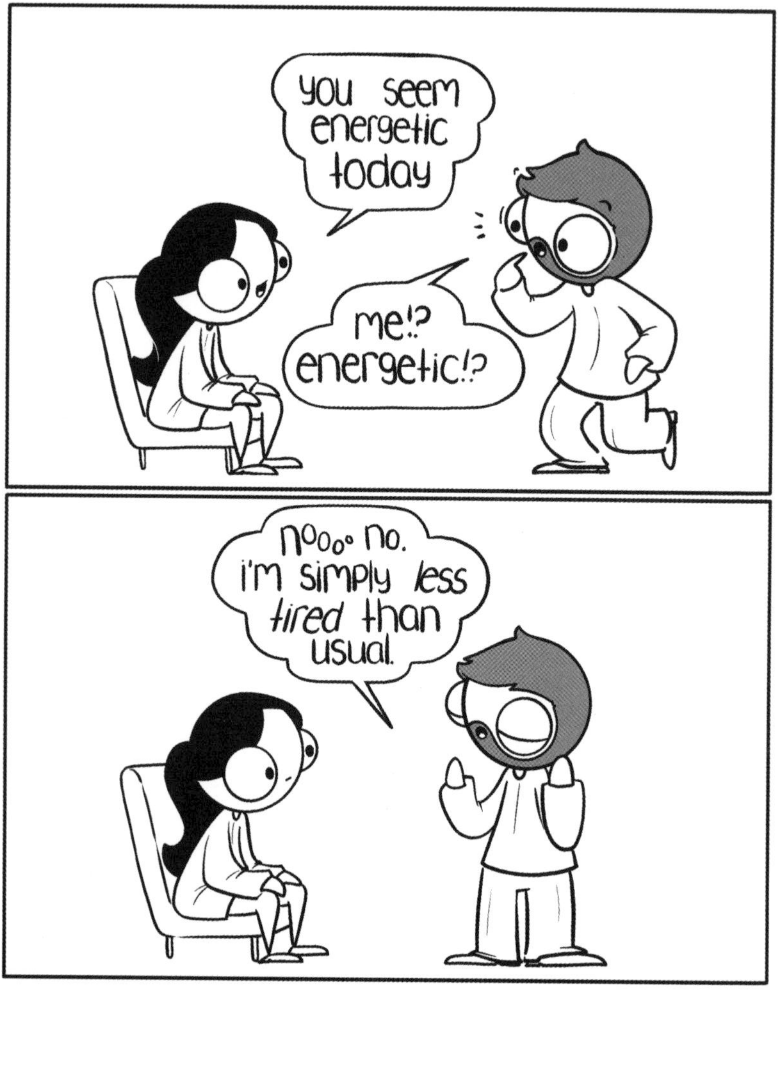
you seem energetic today
me!? energetic!?
nOooo no. i'm simply less tired than usual.

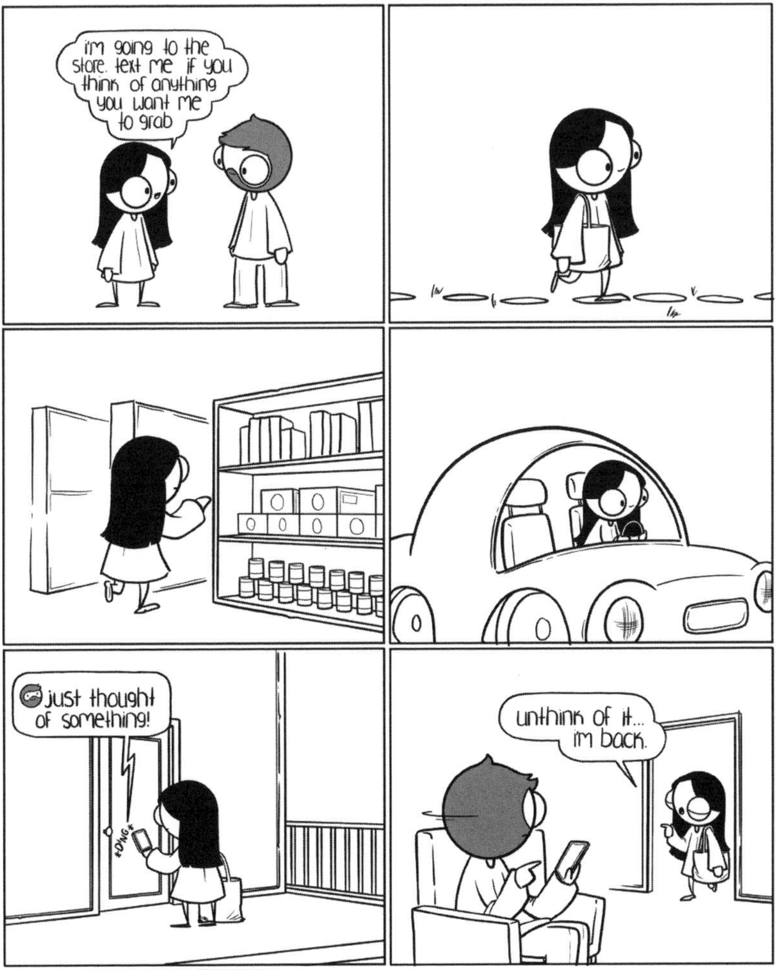
i'm going to the store. text me if you think of anything you want me to grab
just thought of something!
DING
unthink of it... i'm back.

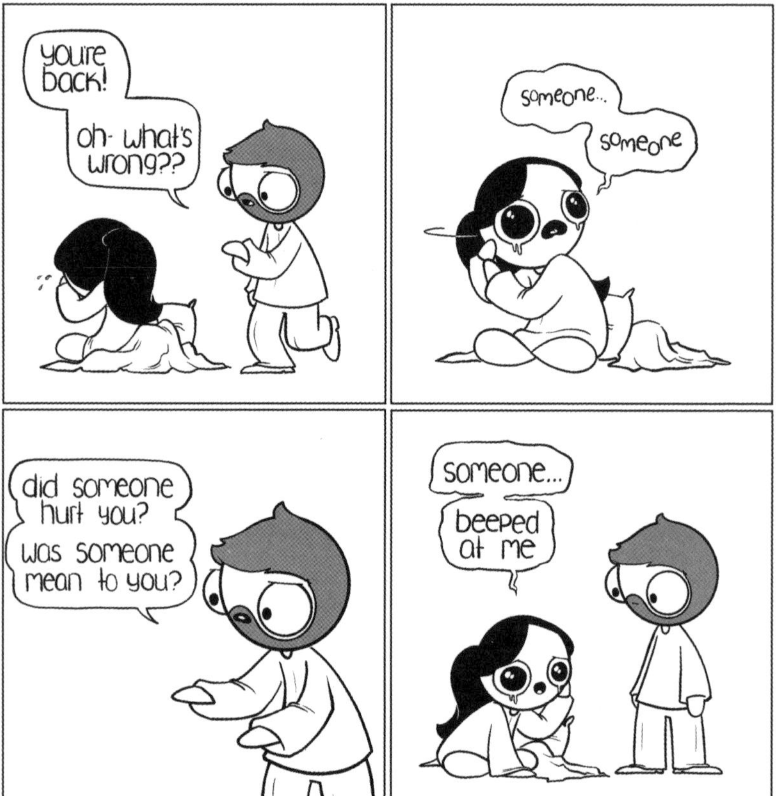
you're back!
oh- what's wrong??
someone...
someone
did someone hurt you?
was someone mean to you?
someone...
beeped at me

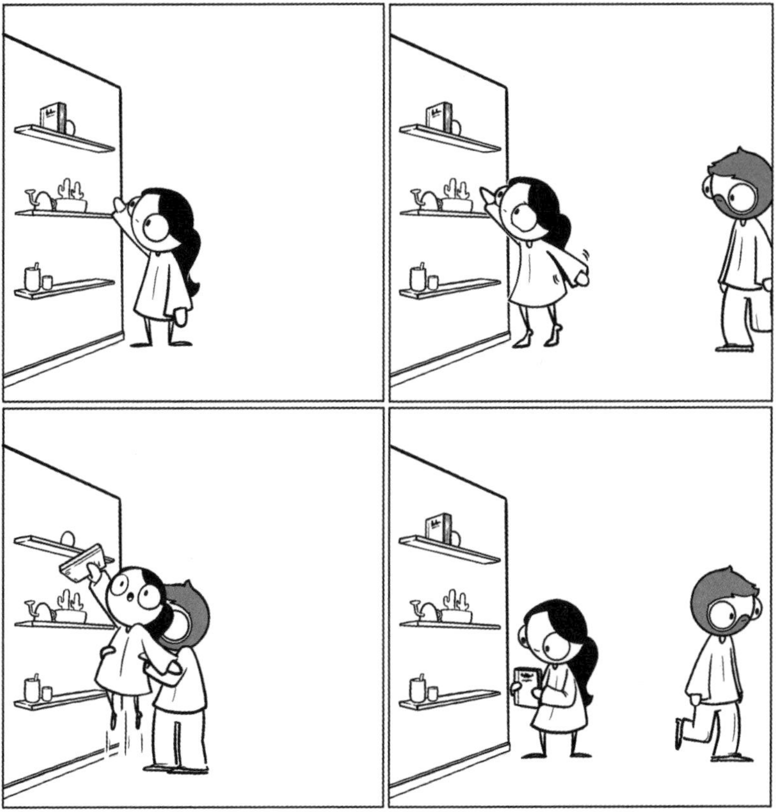

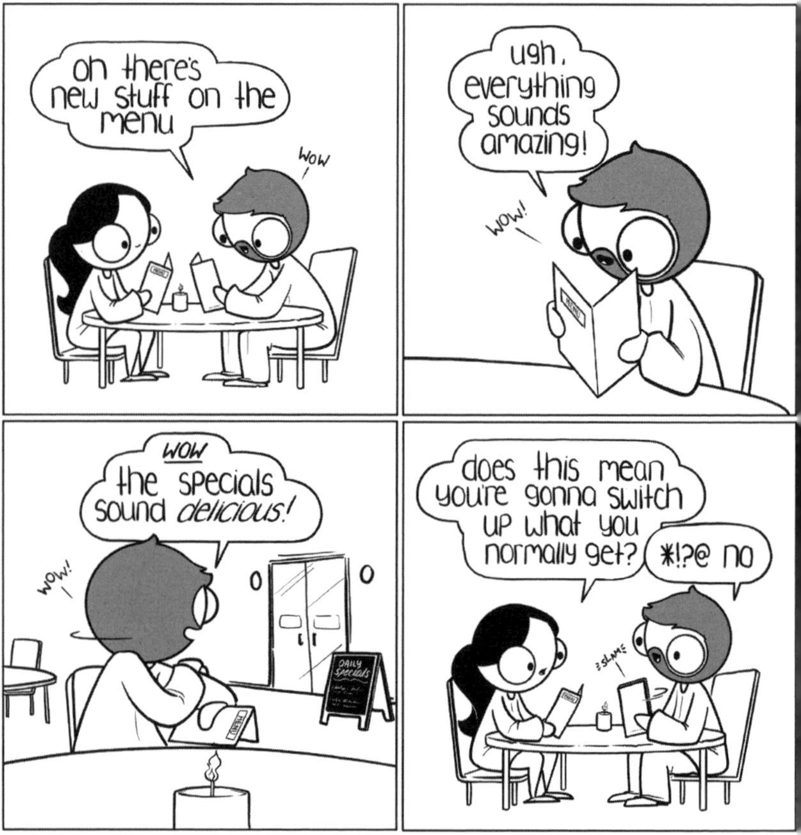
oh there's new stuff on the menu
WOW
MENU
ugh, everything sounds amazing!
WOW!
MENU
WOW
the specials sound *delicious!*
WOW!
DAILY Specials
MENU
does this mean you're gonna switch up what you normally get?
*!?@ no
SLAM
MENU

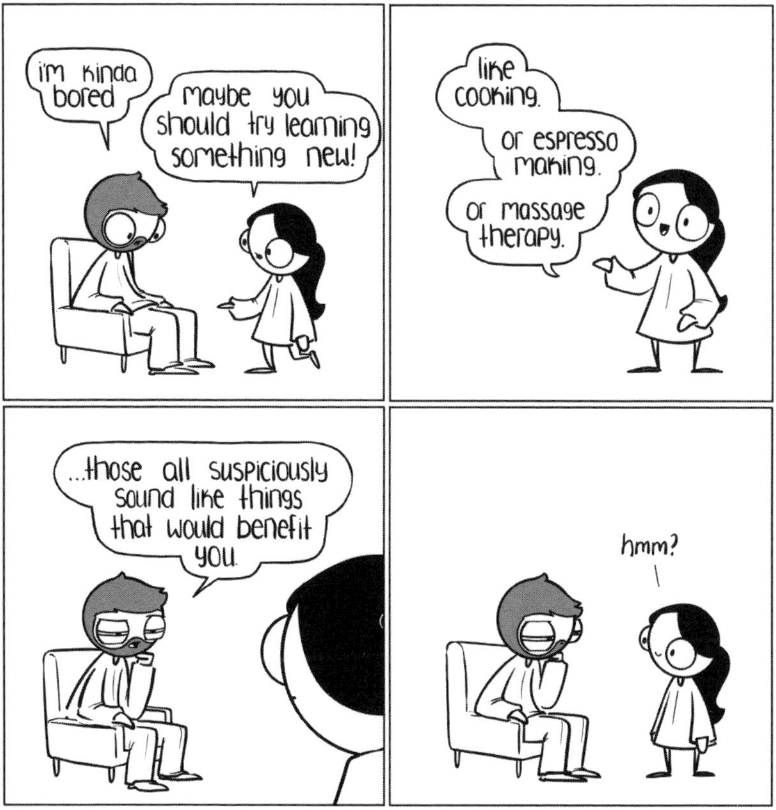
i'm kinda bored
maybe you should try learning something new!
like cooking.
or espresso making.
or massage therapy.
...those all suspiciously sound like things that would benefit you.
hmm?

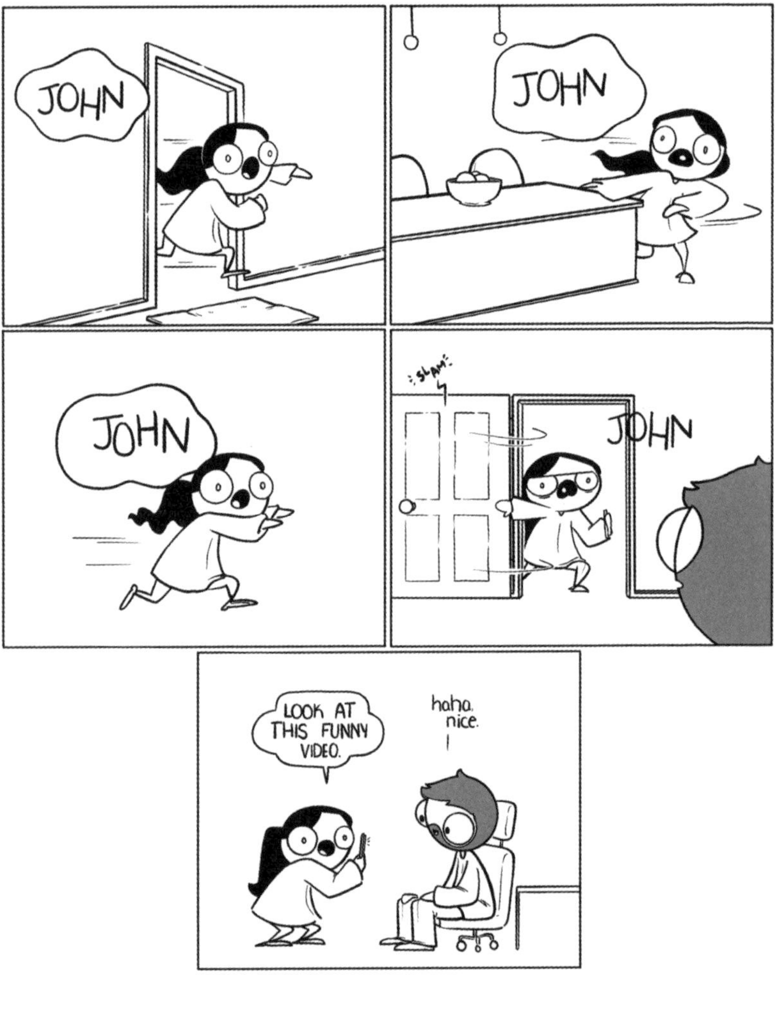
JOHN
JOHN
JOHN
SLAM
JOHN
LOOK AT THIS FUNNY VIDEO.
haha. nice.

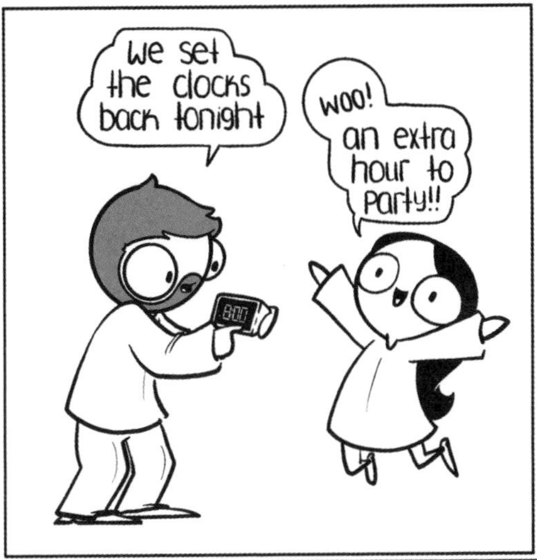
we set the clocks back tonight
woo! an extra hour to party!!

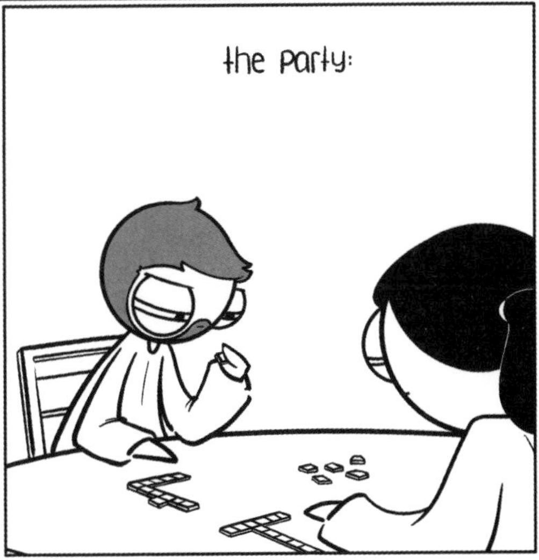
the party:

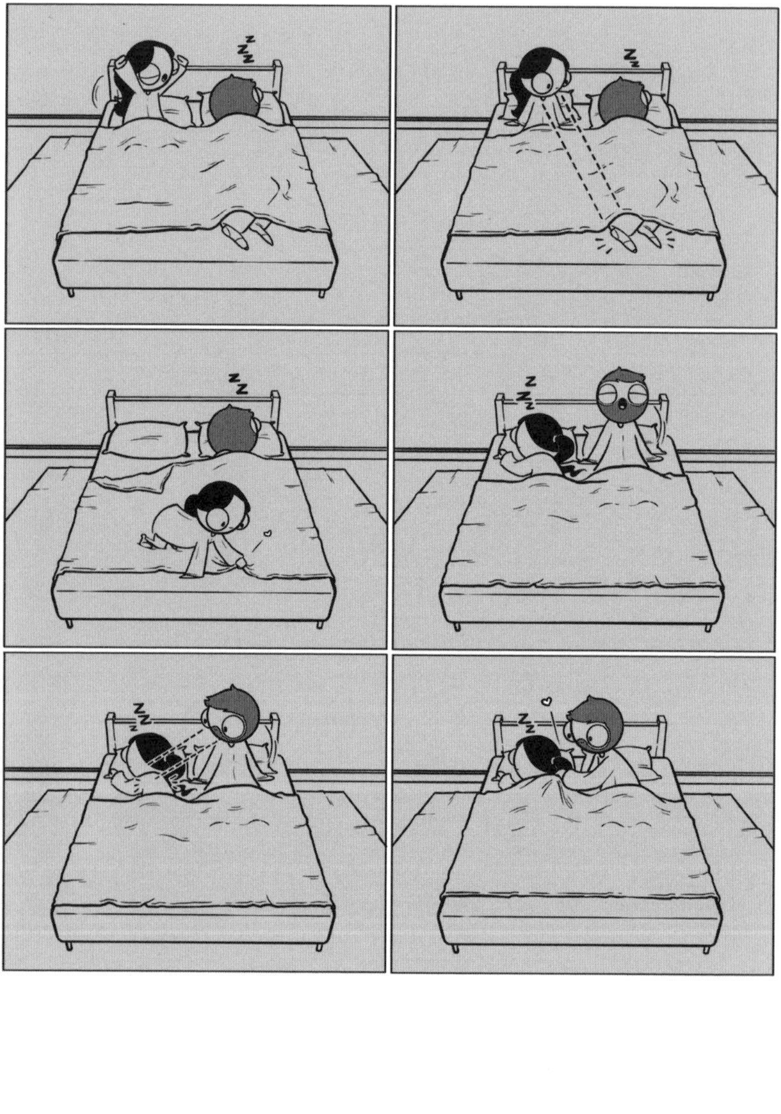

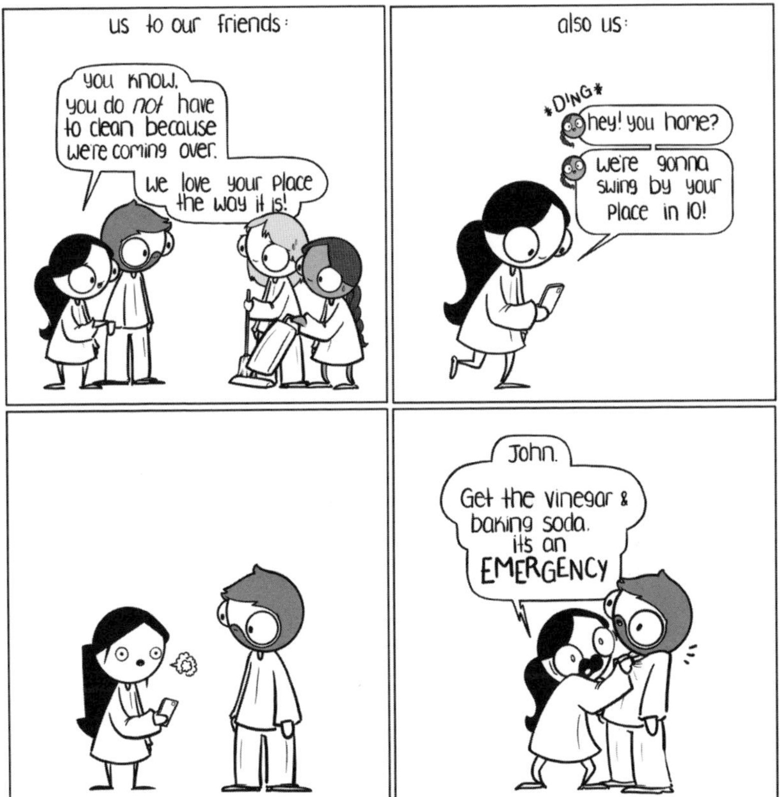
us to our friends:
you know, you do *not* have to clean because we're coming over.
we love your place the way it is!
also us:
DING
hey! you home?
we're gonna swing by your place in 10!
John.
Get the vinegar & baking soda. it's an EMERGENCY

working from home

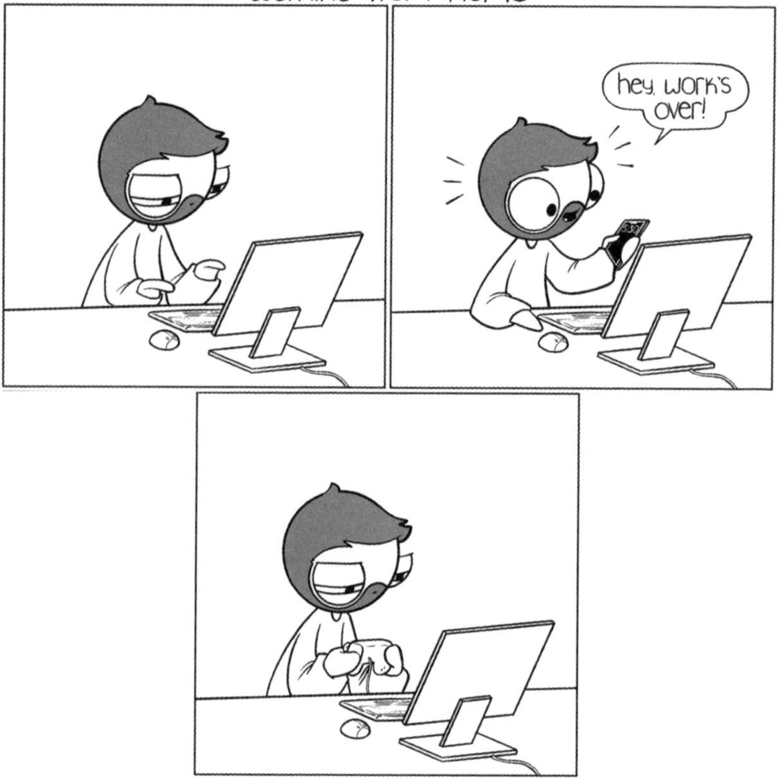
hey, work's over!

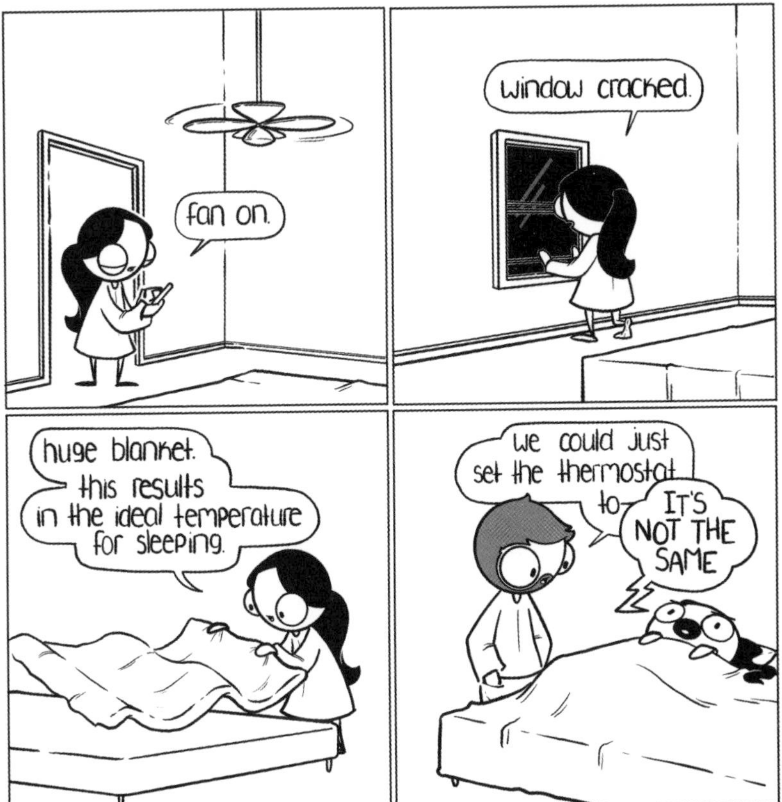
fan on.
window cracked.
huge blanket. this results in the ideal temperature for sleeping.
we could just set the thermostat to-
IT'S NOT THE SAME

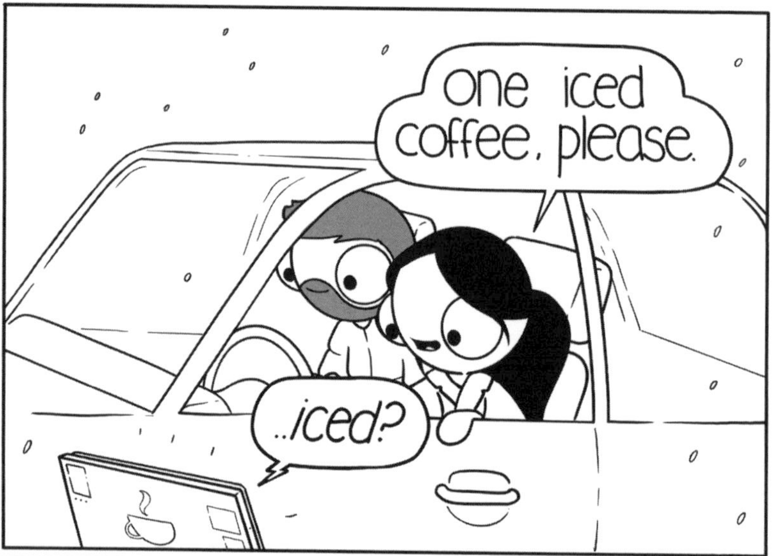
one iced coffee, please.
..iced?

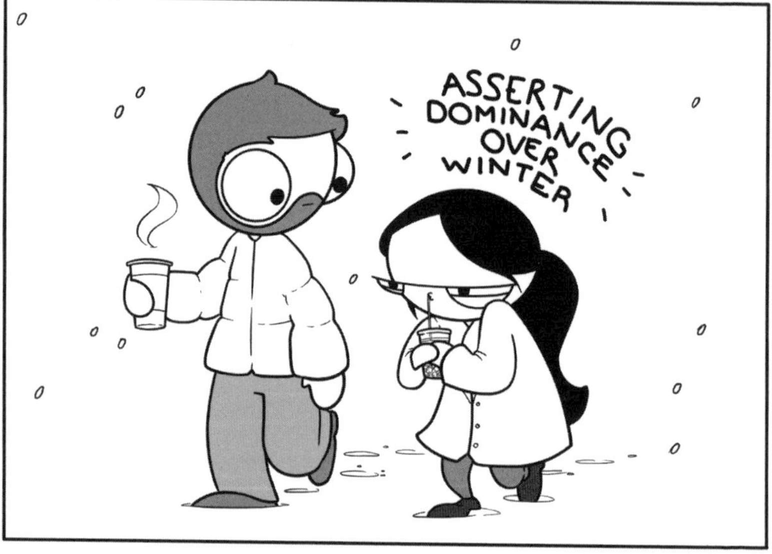
ASSERTING DOMINANCE OVER WINTER

Catana Chetwynd is a self-taught traditional artist and the enthusiastic author of *Catana Comics.* She grew up in Saratoga Springs, New York, where she spent her time creating art and pursuing an education in psychology until accidentally stumbling into the world of comics. Not only is her fiancé, John, the daily inspiration for her drawings, but he was also the one who suggested a comic series about their relationship in the first place. Thanks to his idea and his inspiring daily antics, Catana was able to pursue her childhood dream of being a cartoonist. She currently lives on the East Coast with John and their tiny, angry dog, Murph.

Andrews McMeel Publishing
a division of Andrews McMeel Universal
1130 Walnut Street, Kansas City, Missouri 64106

www.andrewsmcmeel.com

22 23 24 25 26 SDB 10 9 8 7 6 5 4 3 2 1

ISBN: 978-1-5248-7228-1

Library of Congress Control Number: 2022935716

Editor: Patty Rice
Art Director: Holly Swayne
Production Editors: Thea Voutiritsas and Elizabeth A. Garcia
Production Manager: Tamara Haus

ATTENTION: SCHOOLS AND BUSINESSES
Andrews McMeel books are available at quantity discounts with bulk
purchase for educational, business, or sales promotional use. For information,
please e-mail the Andrews McMeel Publishing Special Sales Department:
specialsales@amuniversal.com.

catana comics™

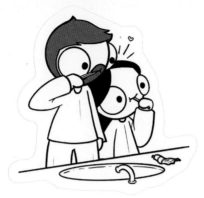

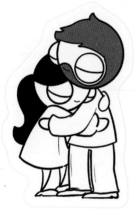

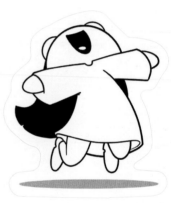

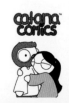

spontaneous
outgoing
impulsive

organized
sensible
intelligent

catana
comics

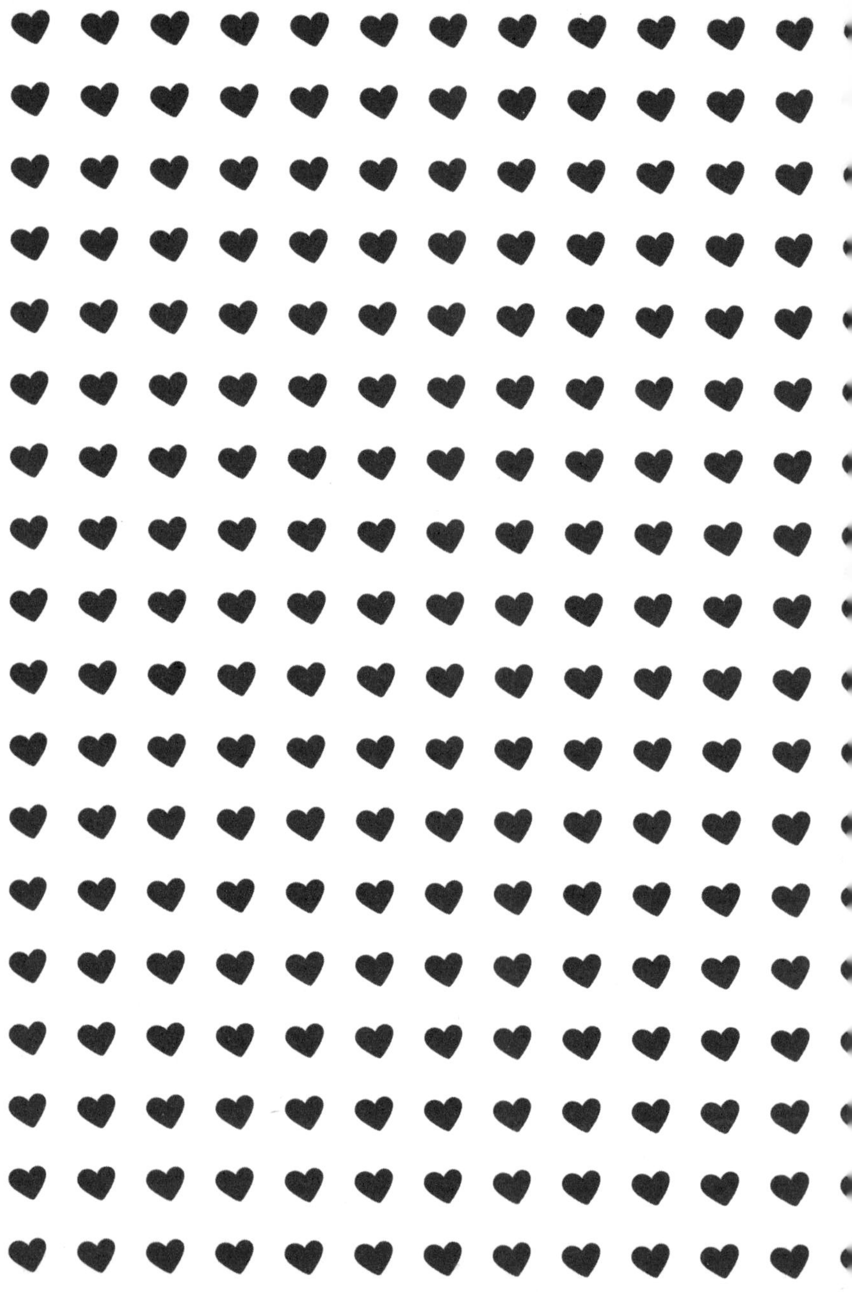